Rock Strata and the Bible Record

Rock Strata and the Bible Record

Edited by
PAUL A. ZIMMERMAN

CONCORDIA PUBLISHING HOUSE
SAINT LOUIS LONDON

Concordia Publishing House, St. Louis, Missouri
Concordia Publishing House Ltd., London, E. C. 1

Library of Congress Catalog Card No. 78-111692

MANUFACTURED IN THE UNITED STATES OF AMERICA

Contents

Preface

Paul A. Zimmerman

This is a book written for the man who in the last third of the 20th century continues to be concerned about the relationship of the truths of the Bible to the truths of science. The authors had in mind the Christian who lives in an age of scientific progress which he respects and who is sometimes troubled by those who assert that this very science has made it impossible to accept as factual many chapters of the Holy Scriptures. In particular he is puzzled about the theory of evolution in its relationship to the Genesis account of creation. What about the fossil record? What do the rocks really tell us? What is the relationship of observed facts to the scientific theories that are built on them? How valid are the conclusions of geology concerning the age of rock strata? How do the actual facts mesh with the Biblical story of man's origin? Is the Bible really mythical in much of its content? Or is it a reliable account of what God really did in His great act of creation? What is the literary genre of the creation account, of the fall of man, of the Flood? What does the New Testament have to say about creation? How old is the earth really? What about Noah's flood? Does modern geology prove that it never happened – that it could not have happened?

A number of men in The Lutheran Church – Missouri Synod in the early sixties felt it would be highly profitable for scientists and theologians to sit around a table and to explore these issues in depth. This conviction led to the appointment of seven men to a study committee which came to be known as the Rock Symposium. It was funded by a grant from the subcommittee on research of the Commission on Church Literature of The Lutheran Church – Missouri Synod.

The members of the Rock Symposium held their first meeting on November 19, 1960. Thereafter the committee met several times each year. Early meetings were devoted to free discussion of points of view, of the assumptions and methodology of science and of theology, and of the issues involved in which science and theology seem to be tangential. Papers were developed touching on the more prominent issues. Eventually the outline of this book took shape. Finally the chapters were written as a summary of the committee's discussion and of important information dealing with the topics assigned to the Rock Symposium.

The chapters that follow do not attempt to present answers to all the questions in this area that trouble the modern Christian. They do not always speak as every member of the symposium would have them speak. Each author is responsible for his own material. But in the main the answers do represent a consensus of the scientists and theologians who probed these questions at meeting after meeting. Above all they do demonstrate what every member of the committee agrees to: The modern Christian can be thoroughly faithful to Christ and to the Holy Scriptures as God's verbally inspired, inerrant Word, without compromising his position as a knowledgeable, competent scientist. He need not compromise either his theological or scientific integrity.

The members of the symposium and their present positions are as follows:

Kenneth L. Currie, Ph. D.; Geological Survey of Canada, Ottawa, Canada

John W. Klotz, B. D., Ph. D.; Professor of Biology, Concordia Senior College, Fort Wayne, Indiana

Fred Kramer, D. D.; Professor of Theology, Concordia Theological Seminary, Springfield, Illinois

Robert D. Preus, Ph. D.; (Secretary) Professor of Theology, Concordia Seminary, St. Louis, Missouri

Wilbert H. Rusch, M. S., Sc. S.; (Chairman) Professor of Biology, Concordia Lutheran Junior College, Ann Arbor, Michigan

Paul C. Tychsen, Ph. D.; Professor of Geology, Wisconsin State University, Superior, Wisconsin

Paul A. Zimmerman, B. D., Ph. D.; President, Concordia Lutheran Junior College, Ann Arbor, Michigan

The members of the Rock Symposium wish to express their gratitude to the following men who attended several of the meetings in a consultant capacity: Dr. James O. Buswell III, Wheaton College, Wheaton, Illinois; Dr. Martin H. Franzmann and Dr. Walter R. Roehrs, Concordia Seminary, St. Louis, Missouri.

In Jesus' Name,

PAUL A. ZIMMERMAN, *Editor*
Ann Arbor, Michigan

SECTION I

Theological and Scientific Guideposts

1 • Guiding Theological Principles

A Lutheran Confessional Approach to the Doctrine of Creation

ROBERT D. PREUS

It has been generally held that there is a uniquely Lutheran hermeneutics. The Lutheran emphasis on the unity of Scripture, the divine origin and authority of Scripture, and the Christocentricity and soteriological aim of all Scripture—all constitute a series of hermeneutical presuppositions of gigantic proportions, presuppositions which will and should totally determine the interpreter's attitude and approach to the sacred Scriptures. Anthropological and soteriological assumptions are also part of the equipment which the Lutheran theologian brings with him as he interprets Scripture. That the exegete is a poor sinner with a habitual inclination toward evil, that he is in constant need of the Spirit's enlightenment, that all his labors to be fruitful must be preceded by earnest prayer, that every thought even of the regenerate reason must be totally subjected to the words and revelation of God, these too are assumptions of sweeping consequence for the exegete as he goes about his task.

It is important that we as Lutherans understand fully these hermeneutical presuppositions which were not only Luther's but were the possession of the entire Lutheran Church for fully two centuries and were fundamental to the Lutheran Symbols in their approach to Scripture. A doctrinal position may well seem like nonsense until we grasp the exegetical method and the canons of hermeneutics which lead to this position. It is particularly important that we know how the writers of our Lutheran Symbols read the Scriptures, inasmuch as we have subscribed to and are committed to the doctrine of these symbols. Certainly, subscribing to the doctrine of the

Lutheran Confessions involves agreement with the basic approach and hermeneutics which were employed by the writers of the confessions in reading Scripture and drawing the doctrine from it. It is important also to know our Lutheran hermeneutics as we study the doctrine of creation; for there is a definitely Lutheran confessional approach to the doctrine of creation, and specifically as it is set forth in Genesis 1 and 2.

May I therefore offer a series of brief observations on the basic hermeneutical principles and the general exegetical procedure of our Lutheran Confessions.

Basic Hermeneutical Presuppositions of the Lutheran Confessions and Procedures for Understanding the Scriptures

The Holy Spirit as the True Interpreter of Scripture

That every Christian needs the grace and enlightenment of the Holy Spirit to understand and believe the Scriptures is an emphasis very strong among Luther and the early reformers. This position is assumed throughout the Lutheran Confessions and is specifically stated in the Formula of Concord which says (SD II, 26): "But to be born anew, to receive inwardly a new heart, mind, and spirit, is solely the work of the Holy Spirit. He opens the intellect and the heart to understand the Scriptures and to heed the Word." In its context this statement shows that the activity of the Spirit in opening up the Scriptures to us is a part of His entire work of converting and enlightening and sanctifying man. It is through the Word that the Spirit comes to us, and it is through the Word—not merely Scriptures, of course, but the Gospel—that He brings us to faith (AC V; Ap XII, 42).[1] This means that only a Christian can read Scripture with complete understanding in the sense of acceptance, although even a Jew or a Turk can often understand the meaning of the words.

The Scriptures as the Word of God Himself

The divine origin, authority, and sufficiency of Scripture are assumed throughout the confessional writings and are a fundamental presupposition to all Lutheran exegesis. This fact is brought out first in those statements which insist that all other writings, even the confessions, are accepted only because they are "drawn from the Word of God" (FC SD Rule and Norm, 10).[2] Again the Word of God is called "eternal truth," and other writings only "a witness to the truth" (FC SD Rule and Norm, 13). Again the Scriptures are called the "pure and clear fountain of Israel," which is the only true norm according to which all teachers and teachings are to be judged and evaluated (FC SD Rule and Norm, Summary Formulation, 3; Epitome, Rule and Norm, 2).

Second, we find the divine origin and authority of Scripture alluded to by many an appeal and obiter dictum in the confessions. When certain Romanists do not face up to the many testimonies in Scripture concerning justification by faith, the question is asked, "Do they suppose that these words fell from the Holy Spirit unawares?" (Ap IV, 108). Speaking of those passages which warn against human traditions and regulations, the question is again asked, "Is it possible that the Holy Spirit warned against them for nothing?" On one occasion the adversaries are faulted for condemning "several articles in opposition to the clear Scripture of the Holy Spirit" (Ap Preface 9). Such passing statements indicate that the divine origin and authority of Scripture was simply assumed, but very consciously so as the writers of the confessions do their exegesis.

Third, the practice in the Lutheran Confessions of citing Scripture faithfully to prove doctrine, of carrying on detailed exegesis where this is deemed necessary, of condemning all adversaries again and again specifically for being unscriptural brings out the importance of the *sola Scriptura* principle for all faithful and serious exegesis. The doctrine of the divine origin and authority of Scripture means that Scripture is inerrant, a fact which is also assumed, as we see in several passing statements within our confessions. The Scriptures are called "eternal truth" (FC SD Rule and Norm, 13). They cannot err or lie to us (LC IV, 57; V, 76).[3] And "God, who is the eternal Truth," does not contradict Himself in Scripture (FC SD XI, 35), for it is His "pure, infallible, and unalterable Word" (Preface to the Book of Concord, p. 8).

The Christocentricity of Scripture and the Law-Gospel Motif

Like a red thread the promises concerning Christ run through the entire Scriptures, giving them a Christological unity and proclaiming one way of salvation (Ap XXIV, 55, 57; IV, 57; XII, 71; cf. also German text). In like manner all of Scripture is said to be distributed into two parts or to teach two works of God in men: Law and Gospel and the work of terrifying and comforting men (Ap IV, 5; XII, 53; FC SD V, 1, 23). Now all Scripture must be read in the light of Law and Gospel, and to confuse the two teachings is to misread Scripture (Ap IV, 218–221). Furthermore, the article of justification as the epitome of the Gospel is the chief theme of all Scripture which must inform the exegete as he goes about his task (Ap IV, 2; German text); otherwise again all is darkness, even though the grammatical sense of Scripture may well be understood by the exegete. A doctrinal unity is maintained by the Lutheran Confessions along with the Christological unity of Scripture, for all Christian doctrine has its center in the doctrine of the Gospel.

The Clarity of Scripture

The clarity of Scripture is maintained by the Lutheran Confessions, and, for the most part, passages of Scripture are cited to support Christian doctrine with little or no comment. This does not imply that there are no obscure passages in Scripture; but again and again the confessions insist that the doctrine taught is based on clear passages of Scripture (Ap IV, 314; LC V, 45; FC SD II, 87; Ap XXIV, 94; FC SD VII, 50; AC XXII, 2; XXIII, 3; XXVIII, 43). Clear passages are those which present no problems in their historical setting or grammatical construction; that which would render any passage or pericope unclear would be either some obscure or unknown historical referent or obscure syntax or vocabulary. Often unclear passages can be explained on the basis of clear passages dealing with the same subject matter.

The Necessity of Grammatical Exegesis; Finding the Literal Sense of Scripture, Which Is One

The exegesis of historic Lutheranism consistently attempts to discern the literal sense, that is, the intended sense, of Scripture passages and pericopes (FC SD, VII, 38, 42, 45 to 48, 50). This is consistent with the humanistic heritage of the day. Therefore the constant question is, What does Scripture say? (Ap IV, 231; 264, 267; XII, 84; 138). What is the intention of the author of any given pericope? To discern this intended meaning of the text all the grammatical, lexicographical, and historical tools of the day were employed. Etymologies, Biblical usage, even extra-Biblical data are brought to bear in the attempt to find the meaning of terms and passages (Ap XXIV, 23, 81–83; FC SD V, 7–9; III, 17; Ap IV, 246–53). The search for the simple and native sense of the passages of Scripture rules out allegorizing of the text, hidden meanings, and fanciful interpretations (Ap XII, 106; XXIV, 35; FC SD VII, 113), and this because *sensus literalis Scripturae unus est.* Any undermining of this basic fact destroys all serious exegesis.

Scripture Interprets Scripture

The principle that Scripture interprets Scripture *(analogia Scripturae)* is derived from the principle of clarity of Scripture and from the fact that the Spirit of God is the principle author of all of Scripture. Therefore any Scripture can shed light on another Scripture passage which deals with the same subject matter; for this is merely interpreting Scripture passages in the light of their widest context. This particular principle is followed by the confessions time and again when they draw from all over Scripture to maintain a certain point (Ap XII, 44–52; IV, 272–285; 256–263; FC SD II, 9–17; 26; VIII, 70). In all such cases various Scripture passages serve to complement each other in offering a complete view of an article of faith. This principle is of especial importance as the exegete interprets unclear passages by clear parallel passages (Ap IV, 87–101; XXVIII, 21; Tr 23 [4]; LC I, 65) and as one interprets and understands Old Testament passages in the light of New Testament interpretation (Ap II, 18, 20; XXIII, 64; XXIV, 36).

The Evangelical Lutheran Hermeneutics as Applied to the Main Themes of Genesis 1–3

There can be little doubt that the Lutheran Confessions (like Luther and the exegetes of the day), regard Genesis 1 and 2 as introducing a history, not presenting a cosmogony. Furthermore, Genesis 2 with its account of Adam and Eve in the Garden cannot be divorced from Genesis 3, which speaks of the fall of these two people into sin. Therefore the entire three chapters are taken together as a unit, although Genesis 3 does not deal specifically with the Creation. One's interpretation of Genesis 3 will notably affect his understanding and interpretation of the preceding chapter. This is very clear in the case of our confessions, which see Genesis 2 in the light of the Fall and the promise of Genesis 3.

Creation

Surprisingly little is said about Creation in the Lutheran Confessions. No cosmogony on the basis of Genesis 1 and 2 is offered, although Luther, Chytraeus, and others in commentaries treat the Genesis account as a plain historical descriptive account or history of what actually took place. There is very little said in the Lutheran Symbols about the creation of the world or the universe. It is rather the theological significance of Creation that is emphasized, and this because of various antitheses of the day. For instance, in contrast to the alleged Manicheism of Flacius the goodness of God's creation is stressed (FC, I). And to defend Luther's doctrine of original sin and total depravity against the charges of Eck and others, the Augsburg Confession, Art. XIX, insists that God is not the cause of sin.

As the Lutheran Confessions treat the many texts dealing with Creation, their discussions seem almost invariably to lead to man as the principal creature of God, just as Genesis 1 must lead to Genesis 2 and is incomplete without it. Man is the creature of a good and beneficent Creator God, and all of God's creation serves man. This is the practical theological significance of Creation and the conclusion to be drawn from the creation account.

> LC, 1st Art. 11-16: If you were to ask a young child, "My boy, what kind of God have you? What do you know about Him?" he could say, "First, my God is the Father, who made heaven and earth. Apart from Him alone I have no other God, for there is no one else who could create heaven and earth."

> For the somewhat more advanced and educated, however, all three articles can be treated more fully and divided into as many parts as there are words. But for young pupils it is enough to indicate the most necessary points, namely, as we have said, that this article deals with creation. We should emphasize the words, "Maker of heaven and earth." What is meant by these words, "I believe in God, the Father almighty, maker," etc.? Answer: I hold and believe that I am a creature of God; that is, that He has given and constantly sustains my body, soul, and life, my members great and small, all the faculties of my mind, my reason and understanding, and so forth; my food and drink, clothing, means of support, wife and child, servants, house and home, etc. Besides, He makes all creation help provide the comforts and necessities of life—sun, moon, and stars in the heavens, day and night, air, fire, water, the earth and all that it brings forth, birds and fish, beasts, grain and all kinds of produce. Moreover, He gives all physical and temporal blessings—good government, peace, security. Thus we learn from this article that none of us has his life of himself, or anything else that has been mentioned here or can be mentioned, nor can he by himself preserve any of them, however small or unimportant. All this is comprehended in the word "Creator."

This statement, which is typical of so many references in our Confessions (AC, XVI, 4–13; FC, Ep I, 2, 4 [5]; FC, SD, I, 34–37), stresses not only the original creation of heaven and earth but also the *creatio continua* (continuing creation) and divine providence of God (FC, SD, XI, 4, 6). The doctrine of creation is *used* to serve man: to humble and terrify us, for we sin daily, but it also serves to lift us up and warm our hearts with gratitude toward God for all His blessings (LC, Creed, I, 22–23).

Adam and Eve

Thus far the exegesis of the Lutheran Confessions pertaining to the doctrine of creation has been application more than interpretation. And this practice is in conformity with that of Scripture itself (Psalm 104; Isaiah 40; Job 38; Col. 1:16 ff.), which uses the doctrine of creation homiletically, doxologically, and polemically. But just as the Scriptures are not using and applying a mere myth, the confessions too, when they apply the doctrine of creation as they do to the needs of their day, in no way minimize the importance of Genesis 1 and 2 as a factual account of a real creation and a *sedes doctrinae* (seat of doctrine). When we observe what our Lutheran Symbols say about Adam and Eve, we notice that more interpretation is offered than application.

There is not the slightest doubt that the confessions receive as actual history and fact the story of Adam and Eve in Genesis 2 (FC, Ep I, 4; SD, I, 9, 27). Adam and Eve were the first two people of this world—placed by God in the Garden of Eden. Adam and Eve were created with body and soul (FC, Ep I, 4), according to Gen. 2:7; they were created in the image of God (according to Gen. 1:27), which consisted in a wisdom and righteousness being "implanted in man that would grasp God and reflect Him, that is, that man received gifts like the knowledge of God, fear of God, and trust in God" (Ap II, 17–18). Here Gen. 2:7 is definitely interpreted according to Col. 3:10 and Eph. 4:24 (*analogia fidei*—analogy of faith). There is no attempt to interpret Gen. 1:27 independently of the New Testament. These two people, Adam and Eve, were originally created pure, good, and holy, as the Genesis account says (FC, SD, I, 27). Furthermore, marriage was established between Adam and Eve, and this cannot be nullified as a God-pleasing institution (AC, XXIII, 8; cf. Matt. 19:4 ff.).

The Fall and Original Sin

We notice here at once that the historical fact of the Fall is never questioned (FC, SD, I, 23, 9); "the dough out of which God forms and makes man has been corrupted and perverted in Adam" (FC, SD, I, 38). We notice also that Satan is the instigator of sin, the one who "corrupted God's handiwork in Adam" (FC, SD, I, 42, 7, 27). In this connection even details connected with the Fall narrative are considered to be factual and historical, such as the devil's manner in tempting Adam and Adam's subsequent contrition (SA III, VIII, 5[6]; Ap XII, 55). For instance, Luther says (SA III, VIII, 5): "All this is the old devil and the old serpent who made enthusiasts of Adam and Eve. He led them from the external Word of God to spiritualizing and to their own imaginations, and he did this through other external words." Third, we notice the connection, alluded to so often (FC, SD, I, 28, 9, 11, 13; Ap II, 5, 2; AC, II, 1), between Adam's sin (fall) and our sinful condition, that since the fall of Adam all men who are propagated according to nature are born in sin (AC II, 1) and that our sin is a hereditary condition (*Erbsünde*) which we have by conception and birth (Ap II, 6, 11, 8, 23). This connection, which is not drawn from Genesis 3 but from Romans 5; Matt. 15:19; Gen. 8:21; 6:5 and other passages, although never explained, is nevertheless real and is an article of faith. Again we notice how the New Testament is simply brought in to interpret the Old Testament. Barth's doctrine of *Ursünde,* that every man is his own Adam, would be totally untenable. In other words, the actuality of the Fall is the basis of the actuality of original sin today. And this is a matter of confession (SA III, I, 1): "Here we must confess what St. Paul says in Rom. 5:12, namely, that sin had its origin in one man, Adam, through whose disobedience all men were made sinners and became subject to death and the devil."

Other facts pertinent to the description of original sin, its guilt, and its punishment are brought out in our Lutheran Confessions, but not on the basis of Genesis 3. It is interesting that in the confessions (FC, I) Genesis 3 (this historical narrative) is the *sedes doctrinae* for the doctrine of the Fall and original sin, and Romans 5 and 1 Corinthians 15 are hardly mentioned.

Conclusions and Comments on the Symbols' Reading and Understanding of the Old Testament on the Themes Treated Above

The interpretation in our confessions of Genesis 1–3 is an ingenuous one which accepts the prima-facie meaning of the story. No hidden, mystical, or allegorical meanings or genres are sought. And, of course, no interpretation of the account in the light of Moses' readership or *Sitz im Leben* is attempted. The matter of the 6 days and their length and other problems which may disturb us today are, of course, not even broached. It is rather the *theological significance* which is emphasized (i. e., 1. a created universe with a transcendent God existing apart from the universe [against pantheism and atheism], 2. a created man and woman as the culmination of God's creation [against polygenesis, which was taught also in those days, e. g., Las Casas, Augustine, Avicenna, and later Isaac Peyrerius], 3. a man created good in the image of God and being immediately at his creation the full realization of what a human is to be [against Manicheism, modern evolutionism, etc.], and 4. a historical fall of Adam and Eve involving an actual act of disobedience against a specific command of God [against minimizing the universality and seriousness of original sin]). We may notice that in all four of these cases other Scriptures can be brought to bear, particularly Romans 5. We note also that the *theological significance* of Genesis 1–3 is for the Lutheran Symbols dependent wholly on the factuality of the account. This means that there is in Genesis 1–3 a description of something actually happening. A nondescriptive account of Genesis 1–3 (e. g., a demythologized poem sung to God's glory; an aetiological saga; a mere cosmology purified of theogony, theomachy, and other unworthy elements; a reworking of various older Hebrew or other myths) would be totally uncongenial to the Lutheran Confessions as being opposed to the serious theological purpose of the section and to the analogy of faith.

Second, it is surprising how little direct attention is given in the Lutheran Confessions (as they deal with the themes above) to Romans 5. Much more attention is directed to Genesis 1–3, which tells the history. We might say that FC, Art. I, deals with original sin on the basis of Genesis 3, with other passages of Scripture brought in to shed light; the entire article is a sort of commentary (polemical, of course) on Genesis 3, or better, a sort of *Gutachten* (theological opinion) based on Genesis 3. Articles II and III of the FC, which deal with the bondage of the will and with justification, are quite different, having no single *sedes,* but roving all over Scripture in presenting the Lutheran position.

We notice finally how clearly operative various hermeneutical rules and assumptions are as our confessions address themselves to the theme of Creation, Adam and Eve, the Fall, and original sin. Clearly we see the confessions seeking the *sensus literalis,* the plain and native meaning, of Genesis 1–3. The principle that Scripture is its own interpreter is constantly assumed and applied, as the analogy of faith is brought to bear upon the Genesis pericope. Belief in the unity of Scripture, both doctrinal and Christological, is apparent throughout, for everything in Scripture dealing with Creation and the Fall is related to the discussion without reservation. Both Creation and Fall are treated in such a way as to lead us to Christ and the Gospel. Again we see all being interpreted in the light of Law and Gospel as the confessions seek to understand and apply the doctrines of the Creation and the Fall (cf. Ap IV, 2, German text).* And we observe that the New Testament interpretation of the Old Testament is taken for granted and accepted without any reservation; the New Testament data are never ignored or lost sight of as Genesis 1–3 is read and applied.

To sum up: the Lutheran Symbols interpret the Biblical themes under discussion both theologically in accord with the evangelical presuppositions for all exegesis and grammatico-historically as the rules of Lutheran hermeneutics would dictate; but in no case do they allow theological assumptions to undermine sound grammatical exegesis. In other words, we would conclude that in their interpretation of Genesis 1–3 our Lutheran Confessions are faithfully following the concerns voiced in the concluding paragraphs of the Formula of Concord, Article XI, 92–93:

> "Whatever was written in former days was written for our instruction, that by steadfastness and by encouragement of the Scriptures we might have hope" (Rom. 15:4). But it is certain that any interpretation of the Scriptures which weakens or even removes this comfort and hope is contrary to the Holy Spirit's will and intent. We shall abide by this simple, direct, and useful exposition which is permanently and well grounded in God's revealed will, we shall avoid and flee all abstruse and specious questions and disputations, and we reject and condemn all those things which are contrary to these true, simple, and useful expositions.

* It cannot be conjectured that Genesis 1–3 has nothing to do with Law and Gospel and that therefore on Lutheran principles (cf. Ap IV, 2, German text) we need not insist on a particular interpretation of this pericope, viz., that it presents a historical fact. The premise of such an allegation is false. It is true that Melanchthon sees the Gospel, epitomized in the article of justification, as the *praecipuus locus* of Christian theology "which is of especial service for the clear, correct understanding of the entire holy Scriptures, and alone shows the way to the unspeakable treasure and right knowledge of Christ, and alone opens the door to the entire Bible" (Ap IV, 2, *Triglot Concordia*); but this article must be seen in the light of God as the "one creator and preserver of all things" (AC I, 3), of man's fall into sin (AC II) and of the redemption of Christ (AC III). Otherwise one falls into some sort of vague antinomianism which in the end tends to vitiate the Gospel as our theological center. It is not by accident that Melanchthon in the AC and in the Apology presents articles antecedent to the central doctrine of justification: God and the creation of all things, the Fall and original sin, Christ and His work of propitiation. All these must be real if there is any reality in the justification of a sinner before God.

Notes

1. AC – The Augsburg Confession; Ap – Apology of the Augsburg Confession

2. FC SD – Formula of Concord, Thorough [Solid] Declaration

3. LC – Large Catechism

4. Tr – Treatise on the Power and Primacy of the Pope

5. FC, Ep – Formula of Concord, Epitome

6. SA – The Smalcald Articles

2 • Assumptions in Science and Paleontology

John W. Klotz

Science is noted for its antiauthoritarianism and for its demand for evidence. Nothing is to be accepted as a fact unless it can be convincingly demonstrated to any inquirer. Modern science has real reason for being proud, because it has insisted on this sort of objectivity. The glory of modern science is the experimental method, the carefully worked out system of test and control which guarantees objective evidence. No Russian needs to believe what American scientists say; he can test their findings in his own laboratory. The history of science is replete with instances of frauds who have been exposed as such because they could not demonstrate to others their reported findings.

Yet there are some fields in which little experimentation is possible: some areas of astronomy, for example, for only to a limited degree can the scientific method be applied in dealing with the broader aspects of this subject. For that reason astronomy is largely descriptive and theoretical. Another of these areas in which experimentation is of limited applicability is the area under consideration, paleontology. It is not possible to apply to the past the rigid tests which can be applied to phenomena on our time level. Consequently a study of the past does not give the degree of validity and reliability that a study of phenomena on our time level yields. William S. Beck, in his *Modern Science and the Nature of Life* says, "When all is said and done, there seems to be evidence that even the 'laws of nature' are changing. Modern physics suggests the possibility that changes are taking place in the speed of light and the rates of chemical reactions. In other words, the universe is changing, and it becomes hazardous to attempt calculations concerning the very remote past and the future."[1] Scientists cannot speak with certainty of the past, and this lack of validity and reliability is a part of the nature of the problem. This fact has often been overlooked, and the consequence is that many people assign to scientific statements regarding the past a higher degree of reliability and validity than is justified.

It might also be pointed out that scientists are not quite as objective as they say they are. It is simply not possible for the scientist to detach himself completely from the theories and hypotheses which he espouses. This is particularly true when they are different or new. He finds considerable pride of authorship and an intense personal loyalty to ideas which he has developed. For this reason there is a great deal of subjectivity in science. It is not possible for the scientist to withdraw himself completely from the system which he is observing. He is a part of the system, and consequently some of his judgments are likely to be subjective.

But there is another aspect to this problem, and that is that many of the statements and observations are made on assumptions, the correctness of which is not always sufficiently examined. Indeed philosophers suggest that this is the contribution they can and would like to make to modern science, and they report that this service of theirs is sometimes spurned. Actually, of course, assumptions by their very nature cannot be proved or disproved, yet often this is not recognized. Textbooks, especially those prepared for introductory courses, frequently fail to call attention to the assumptions they are making. The assumptions made are presumably the most logical ones, and it is quite likely that they are fruitful in scientific studies, but they are still assumptions, and must be recognized as such.

Moreover, we cannot ignore the point of view of a given period of time. Assumptions that appear logical and are actually productive today may one day be replaced. The Ptolemaic point of view with its assumptions was both logical and helpful, but it has been replaced with the Copernican point of view. The phlogiston theory of combustion rested upon a series of logical assumptions and produced results, but it too has now been replaced.

Perhaps the most common assumption in dealing with

rock strata and the fossil record is the assumption of uniformitarianism. Lyell, who introduced this concept, conceived the past as very similar to the present; hence the present form of the earth, he believed, had arisen by the long-continued action of forces operating in the same way and at the same rate as they now act.

Darwin himself was greatly influenced by Lyell. Until the middle of the 19th century most paleontologists were catastrophists. They believed that the rock strata could best be explained by assuming that the world had undergone a series of catastrophies which accounted for the strata and their unique fauna. This was the assumption of the day, and it seemed to work. Perhaps the outstanding exponent of this point of view was Cuvier who dominated paleontology in the late 18th and early 19th centuries. Cuvier was a brilliant man, and many of his deductions were truly remarkable. Cuvier was a catastrophist. He believed that life had been wiped out at various times by a series of catastrophies. He suggested that after each of these catastrophies the world was repopulated by animals from some undisturbed part of the earth. Catastrophism has always had an appeal to those who have been interested in reconciling science with the Genesis account. For one thing, the Flood itself fits in with the general philosophy of catastrophism. And there have been those who have modified the ideas of Cuvier and his followers to postulate a series of creations by God following a series of divinely sent catastrophies. Those who support the hiatus interpretation (gap theory) of Genesis 1 also tend to accept catastrophism.

Much of paleontology today is based on evolution, and evolution was based historically on the principle of uniformitarianism. Cuvier's followers have been all but completely routed. There are few today who will accept the catastrophism which Cuvier postulated. Lyell's dictum is popularly accepted by those who would regard themselves as faithful: everything we see in the rock record is the result of natural processes going on over a period of many years and operative today.

Yet today catastrophism has been reintroduced in a modern form, and the pendulum has swung away from strict uniformitarianism. This was apparent from discussions carried on at the 1963 meeting of the Geological Society of America, where Dr. Norman Newall proposed junking both terms: catastrophism and uniformitarianism, because he said they were both too confusing. Still in many textbooks, particularly in introductory courses and in popularizations of geology, it is still essentially Lyell's uniformitarianism that is presented.

Closely allied to uniformitarianism is the principle of uniformity. There are various definitions of this. Most people identify the principle of uniformity with the idea that all observable phenomena can be explained on the basis of natural laws and of cause-and-effect relationships, and that known scientific laws hold throughout time and space. This permits a modicum of catastrophism, but it does insist on the rule of natural law. In this connection, Dr. Beck's statement regarding changes in the laws of nature, referred to earlier, is most interesting.

It is probably worth pointing out that the Christian approach to a study of science would suggest acceptance of the principle of uniformity. Our God is a God of order: He is not a capricious God whose ways can never be studied or predicted. He does perform miracles, but ordinarily He works through the orderly laws He has established.

Uniformity and uniformitarianism are often confused. There is still a great deal of the old uniformitarianism not only in geology but also in geochemistry. It is basic to time studies that are made with the uranium time clock or with carbon-14. Yet it should be recognized that uniformitarianism in the sense that processes have gone on in the past at the same apparent rate at which they are going on at present is an *assumption,* and that by its very nature it cannot be proved. It may be valid in scientific reasoning, since the alternatives to it are less acceptable, inasmuch as without this assumption no conclusions at all can be reached. It is reasonable to assume that processes went on in the past at the same apparent rate and in the same way in which they are going on at present unless we have clear evidence that they were different. Thus it seems valid to assume that uranium has decayed at a fixed rate throughout time. The burden of proof must be with those who challenge it.

At the same time we must recognize philosophically that

it is an assumption and nothing more. We should also recognize that from a philosophical standpoint it is *unlikely* that processes have always gone on in the same way and at the same rate at which they go on at present. Caullery, a well-known French biologist, speaks of the interesting possibility that the natural laws of today may not have applied rigorously throughout the vast stretches of geological time.[2] Beck says the same thing. Uniformity and uniformitarianism are assumptions and nothing more.

In dealing with assumptions such as uniformity and uniformitarianism we ought to recognize that there is a hierarchy of reliability. It would seem reasonable to assume that the laws which govern the universe are uniform in time and space; the alternative would make scientific studies useless. However the uniformity of rates of scientific processes is of a different level: many factors affect rates, and we cannot be sure we have taken all of these into consideration.

Another assumption of most paleontologists is that the absence of a fossil form in association with related forms from the rocks of a given geological period is evidence that the organism did not exist at the period of time when the strata were laid down. This is the basis for the evolutionary concept of development from simple to complex. Incidentally, Kerkut in his *Implications of Evolution* believes there is no such evidence except in the mammals and postulates a polyphyletic origin of living things[3]—which is essentially what Genesis teaches. Yet the generally accepted concept is that of a phylogenetic tree which requires relatively simple organisms and few of them in the early rocks and more complex organisms later. It is argued that these more complex organisms did not exist during the early history of the earth because we do not find their fossils in these early strata. It is also argued that the trilobites dominated in Cambrian times because their fossils are more abundant, that insects dominated in Carboniferous times and that reptiles dominated in Mesozoic times because their fossils are most abundant in these periods.

We are finding more and more organisms that occur earlier than they were once thought to occur. In fact there is good reason for believing that most phyla were present in

Cambrian times. There is even some suggestion that fish were present already in this period. Today more and more forms are being found even in pre-Cambrian rock.

The absence of a fossil form does not necessarily indicate absence of the organism under consideration. The assumption that absence indicates it did not exist at this time can be shown to be wrong not only on the basis of logic but also on the basis of observation. It is illogical to assume that the absence of a form from a given rock stratum *proves* that it did not exist at that time: it may not have existed; it may have existed and not been fossilized; it may have been fossilized and not yet been discovered.

But there is also observational evidence which shows this assumption wrong. The coelocanth, a lobe-finned fish which was discovered in 1937, is an example of this. Until it was taken off the coast of Madagascar in that year it was believed that the crossopterygians were extinct. The coelocanth itself was believed to be extinct for from 50 million to 120 million years. Now, why was it believed to be extinct? It was because it was unknown in the fossil record for that long a time. The last fossils of this form were known from rocks which geologists claimed were anywhere from 50 to 120 million years old.

Nor is this the only example of the discovery of a "living fossil." The Metasequoia (dawn redwood) was believed to have been extinct for 20 million years, again because its fossils were unknown from rocks that were younger. Yet in 1944 it was found alive in the interior of China and since that time an entire grove of these trees has been found. Seeds have been collected, and we have some of these trees growing now in the United States.

A more recently discovered "fossil" was the Neopolina, a supposedly extinct mollusc that was dredged up in connection with studies carried on during the International Geophysical Year. This form was believed to have been extinct for 200 million years, again because its fossils were unknown from younger rocks.

These discoveries of living fossils are significant, not because we may expect to find dinosaurs still alive in some remote corner of the globe or because the continuing discovery of supposedly extinct forms will reduce substantially the number of forms which are truly extinct, but rather in showing how hazardous it is to argue that a form did not exist during a period in which its fossils are not found in the rocks. This assumption is a tenuous one indeed.

Another assumption of much popular reasoning in evolution is that the fossil record is representative and that a representative sample of the organisms which existed during a given geological period has been preserved. Now as a matter of fact everyone recognizes that the fossil record is not a random sample; it is a highly selected sample. Yet much of the reasoning in evolution is constructed as if it were representative. The fact of the matter is that most fossils come from shallow seas, swamps, lagoons, and flood plains. It is here that fossilization is assumed most likely to take place. Immediate burial is needed, and this burial must exclude air so as to prevent oxidation of the remains. It is in the shallow seas and swampy areas that we have this condition best met. We have less fossil evidence of life in deep water because these areas are just becoming available for study. Deep sea basins are regarded as permanent and have not been uplifted so that we may examine them. It is only when an area is uplifted that we can examine its fossil record in detail. Thus for a study of the deep seas we must depend on cores which provide only a very limited picture. We also have less evidence of life that existed on the plains and prairies and mountains because the organisms that lived and died here rarely left fossils. Occasionally one of them drowned and his body was covered with silt in a river, but these fossils are much less common than the fossils of organisms which lived in the shallow seas or swamps. It is true that we have a few organisms from such famous traps as the La Brea tar pits, but these too are unusual and rare.

The fact of the matter is that the fossil record is not random. We have very little evidence of the type of life found in a large number of habitats. We know rather well the life of shallow seas and lagoons, but who would want to insist that these same forms were found in the uplands, on prairies, and on mountains? It may be that the plants and animals of these habitats were quite different; indeed it may be that if we knew them we would regard them as quite advanced. In Pennsylvanian times for example, practically all the known terrestrial plants are those which lived in swamps and marshes or immediately surrounding them. Very little is known of the upland vegetation of that period.

Another area that deserves reexamination is the subject of index fossils. Certain species are said to be index fossils because they are believed to be uniquely characteristic of a given period of time. They may not necessarily be common but they are regarded as unique and limited to a given time. These help to date the rocks and correlate rock structure from area to area and continent to continent. This technique assumes that in the particular period the fossil form was uniformly present over broad areas.

Today we do not have many forms that have worldwide distribution in their ecological niches. The killer whale, the arctic tern, and some mosquitoes are reasonably so. It is difficult to believe that in past times forms were frequently universal in their distribution in their ecological niche. Indeed it seems logical to assume that forms differed in their abundance at different times in different parts of the earth. They can be used to correlate the rocks only if they are abundant enough to form a discoverable number of fossils and used to date the rock only if they appear and disappear simultaneously over a broad area. Forms abundant at a given time may be helpful in dating and correlating rocks over small areas, but it is very hazardous to assume close to a worldwide distribution for the index fossils.

The study of the fossil record tends to ignore the tremendous influence that the environment may have on an organism. It is difficult to measure the effect of the environment, but there is no doubt that the environment brings about substantial changes and modifications. These are of no evolutionary significance because they do not affect the organism's germ plasm. We are all familiar with the twisted elfin timber that we find close to timber line. Here the trees are stunted and gnarled. Yet if the acorn from an oak growing in this habitat is removed and planted in a protected valley it will assume a shape quite different from that of the parent form. Bonnier's experiments and those of Clements, Martin, and Long give some indication of the tremendous influence of the environment. Bonnier reported that sea-level species planted in the mountains came to resemble the mountain species so closely as to be indistinguishable from them.[4] Clements, Martin, and Long go so far as to claim the conversion of one genus into another by changes in altitude.[5] The bonsai trees (miniature trees), correctly the pride of many horticulturalists, are another example of the profound effect of an altered environment.

The effect of environment in animals is well known. The skeletal system, which is the one the paleontologist must work with, is particularly liable to environmental modification. It may be changed by disease. This is what happens in such a disorder as bovine tuberculosis, which fortunately is quite rare today. This disorder, contracted from impure milk, causes the typical spine deformation which we find in a hunchback. The skeleton may be modified by a dietary deficiency: people are taller today not because they are different from the humans of the Middle Ages, but because they are better fed. At one time rickets was quite common in children deprived of milk or of Vitamin D. This disorder caused a twisting of the bone which left permanent deformation. The individual may suffer some endocrine disorder. His pituitary may manufacture too much of the growth hormone and he will be a pituitary giant, or his endocrine system may go awry after he has fully matured and he suffers from acromegaly.

All of these conditions substantially and markedly affect the skeletal system. Yet the effect of the environment is sometimes ignored in paleontology. It may be assumed that the fossil forms found in the rocks have grown up under normal conditions. Obviously it is difficult to measure the effect of the environment of the past. However, assuming that it has had *no* substantial influence leaves much to be desired.

As a result of this and other assumptions there has probably been an unnecessary multiplication of genera and species in the fossil record. Paleontologists have tended to emphasize differences and minimize similarities.

This same tendency to multiply the number of named forms is present in any area of taxonomy at the beginning of the study of a group. The birds are probably a good example of this. In 1910 there were 19,000 species of birds listed. Since that time 8,000 additional forms have been recorded. Yet careful study has actually reduced the number of species, and ornithologists today record only 8,500 species of birds. The general tendency in all taxonomy today is to reduce the number of named species; modern taxonomy favors the lumpers.

The paleontologist has a special problem in that he cannot apply one of the critical tests of determining good species, the breeding test. No doubt this has complicated his work and has been responsible for some of the extravagant naming of species. Careful studies have been applied to only a few fossil forms. The reason for this is the large number of fossil forms which remain unstudied. Our museum storerooms are literally jammed with fossils, still crated, which curators and their assistants have been unable to examine. Added to this has been the large amount of material in the field which must be studied. It is understandable that there is pressure to collect and study. Fossil material that is exposed is soon eroded and destroyed. The limited paleontological resources available are largely directed toward collecting, cataloging, and describing. There is little time for really careful studies and comparisons.

This has led to an unnecessary multiplication of forms. There is the natural tendency to emphasize differences and minimize similarities. The careful comparisons that should be made are not made—simply because there is not the time to make them. One cannot help but be impressed by what has happened as a result of the careful study of human fossil forms. Here we have a paucity of materials, and this very paucity makes it easier to study and compare them. In addition there is a natural interest in a study of human and allegedly prehuman forms. The results of these careful studies have been rather striking. The forms are not so different from modern man and from each other as the names which their discoverers employed would seem to indicate. Today there is general agreement that the Neanderthal and Cro-Magnon man are *Homo sapiens.* The supposedly brutish Neanderthal is not nearly so different from modern man as early descriptions indicated, and in average brain size the Cro-Magnon man and some of the Neanderthalers actually exceeded modern man.

But these studies have even gone farther. Weidenreich does not believe that the South African forms, *Australopithecus,* are ancestral to man. Excluding them, he says that all prehistoric forms are *Homo sapiens.* In this statement he includes *Pithecanthropus* (Java man), *Sinanthropus* (Pekin man), and other early forms. Ernst Mayr does not go so far. He believes that there are three species represented. In the first of these he includes *Pithecanthropus* and *Sinanthropus* and calls it *Homo erectus.* In the second he includes the South African forms, naming these *Homo transvaalensis.* All other forms he classifies as *Homo sapiens.* Even his classification is important and significant to us, for he places all these forms into one genus, *Homo,* and believes there are only two species different from modern man.

The studies of both Weidenreich and Mayr were completed before Leakey's discoveries in Tanganyika, but it is interesting to note that Leakey names a recent discovery *Homo habilis* and that he seems to have eliminated *Zinjanthropus* (Nutcracker man) from the list of man's ancestors.

It is possible that a careful study of all fossil forms might lead to a similar reduction in the number of named species.

Still another assumption that is basic to much of evolutionary paleontology and indeed to much general evolutionary reasoning is the assumption that similarity is a function of descent and that degree of similarity is a measure of the closeness of the common ancestor. In a sense this argument has something to recommend it. It is true that siblings, brothers and sisters, do resemble one another. Members of the same family do look alike. But the evolutionist uses the argument in a little different way. He makes a logical jump from the statement that those who are related tend to look alike to the statement that those who look alike are related.

This is not to say that resemblances are in no way indicative of relationships. But it should be pointed out that there are many facts which throw serious doubt on the validity of this assumption. The evidence from parallel mutations is impressive. The *Drosophila* evidences show us very clearly that similar traits need not have originated from a common ancestor. *Drosophila* is the small fruit fly widely used in genetic studies. In *Drosophila melanogaster* and *Drosophila simulans* there have been eye mutations to prune, ruby, and garnet; body color mutations to yellow; bristle shape mutations to forked and bobbed; and wing mutations to crossveinless, vesiculated, and rudimentary. Two fruit flies showing the same trait need not have acquired it from a common ancestor. It has been argued that the fact of parallel mutations is itself an argument in favor of evolution—that these mutations have occurred only because the germ plasm of the two species was so similar. But this is not the point. The fact of the matter is that a prune-eyed *Drosophila melanogaster* and prune-eyed *Drosophila simulans* have *not* inherited that eye color from a common ancestor; they have inherited that trait from different ancestors.

The situation is even clearer in the various cases of albinism that occur. This trait is rather common, not only in the animal kingdom, but even in the plant kingdom. Those who display it need not have gotten it from a common ancestor. Moreover, there is little doubt from albinism studies that this trait can be brought about in different ways. The end result is the same, but the way in which it is accomplished in two separate organisms may be different. Two organisms which show this trait may well have gotten it from different ancestors; it is hard to argue that this is an evidence for descent from a common ancestor.

Moreover the evolutionist selects his resemblances. Those which suit his theories of descent are emphasized: those which do not suit are ignored. It is to this that Dobzhansky refers when he says that in the present natural system of classification the lines of separation between the systematic categories have been adjusted at least in theory not so much to the discontinuities observed as to the branching of real or assumed phylogenetic trees.[6] Thus the natural system of classification is set up on the basis of supposed evolutionary relationships, and then it is used to prove evolution.

There are a great many resemblances which are ignored because they do not fit with supposed evolutionary developments. Perhaps a classical example of this is the duckbill or platypus. The animal not only has a duck-like bill: it also has webbed feet and tarsal spurs and lays eggs. If the evolutionist thought this animal was related to the Anatidae (ducks), these similarities would probably be stressed. These similarities would be regarded as clear evidences of an evolutionary relationship. But because the duckbill is classified as a monotreme (a low order of mammal) and is not supposed to be closely related to the ducks, these similarities are ignored.

Another relationship that is ignored is that between the extinct woolly rhinoceros and the living white rhinoceros of Africa. Both tooth and skull structures are similar, yet they are separated taxonomically because it is believed they have descended from separate ancestors.

The evolutionist very conveniently argues that similarities which do not fit his theories have developed by convergence. He believes that different animals in the same environment develop similar characteristics. Thus if the similar traits are needed to prove relationship, they are used to do just that; if similarities prove the wrong thing, they are explained as being due to convergence. Kerkut believes that except for the vertebrates there are not enough similarities to prove monophyletic development; he believes rather that the evidence indicates a polyphyletic development of most forms.[7]

It is also worth commenting on the value and significance of the various restorations which we find in our museums. It is not so easy to put muscle on bone as these restorations would lead us to believe. Nor is it as easy to reconstruct a whole animal from a single or a few bones as some would have us believe. In some cases, where we are fortunate, we have an entire skeleton preserved as a fossil. This gives us some information, but by no means all the information we would like to have. We do not really know how these animals looked in the flesh. One of the dinosaurs, *Stegosaurus,* for instance, has a series of vertical triangular bony plates on his back. We do not really know how this animal looked in the flesh, for we do not really know what function these bones served. In one of the reconstructions that has been made, the plates are paired; in another they are nicely arranged in an alternating fashion. Some think they were armor plates: others question their value for protection and suggest they were a frightening device to make *Stegosaurus* look larger than he really was. In any case they are thought to have been a real physiological drain on the reptile when they were growing and attaining full size.[8]

A similar situation holds with regard to reconstructions of the pelycosaurs such as *Dimetrodon*. These carnivores had a specialized "sail" coming up out of their backs. Actually these bones looked very much like the palings of a fence. All sorts of suggestions have been made as to their function and of course assumed function determines the reconstruction. It has been suggested that these served to protect against savage enemies who might become impaled on them. But this seems unlikely since there were no other active carnivores at this time. Others have suggested that these may have been heat-radiating devices which aided in the control of internal temperature. Some have suggested that these were recognition marks. Some have regarded them as sails used when the reptiles ventured out on lakes and rivers and still others have said they were the product of an unbalanced growth pattern and hence had no function.[9]

Hooton, the well-known Yale anthropologist who died a few years ago, has some very interesting things to say about reconstruction of fossil men. He says that because the faces are usually missing, reconstruction of the facial skeletons leaves room for a great deal of doubt as to details. To attempt to reconstruct the soft parts is an even more hazardous undertaking. The lips, the eyes, the ears, and the nasal tip leave no clues on the underlying bony parts. Hooton says that you can model on a Neanderthal skull either the features of a chimpanzee or those of a philosopher. He concludes by saying that the alleged restorations of ancient types of man have very little, if any, scientific value and are likely only to mislead the public.[10]

It is extremely difficult to reconstruct forms from a few bones. The man who gained the reputation of being able to do this was Cuvier, to whom we have deferred earlier. Though he never claimed this ability for himself, people generally believed that he had the ability to restore a whole animal from one fragment of bone.

We are not arguing here that it is impossible to restore a single missing bone. We are pointing out that it is not possible to restore a whole animal from one fragment of bone. Obviously it is proper to supply missing bones, especially if these are known from another specimen. This is common practice in restorations in museums. But it is hardly likely that anyone can reconstruct an entire form from a single bone or just a few bones.

It is of course true that a great deal can be learned from a single human bone. It is often possible to predict quite accurately the age, sex, height, and weight of the individual from whom it has come. This is possible because thousands of measurements have been made on living humans. This information is important and valuable when unidentified remains are discovered. But it is not possible to predict what the individual looked like; from a single femur you cannot draw a sketch of the individual and then match that against photographs of missing persons.

Moreover, the predictions we are able to make from a single human bone are only possible because thousands of measurements have been made on human beings. In the case of most of the fossils, we do not have living organisms which we can measure and against which we can make comparisons. Accurate restorations of extinct forms from one or a few fossil bones are simply not possible. Simpson classifies this supposed ability as "folklore." He says that this ability is ascribed to paleontologists to their distress. He criticized many of the restorations that have been made and says that a prudent paleontologist is sometimes appalled at the extent of restoration indulged in by anthropologists.[11]

Another assumption that is widely employed is the assumption that extrapolation—estimating beyond the known range on the basis of certain variables within the known range—is valid as evidence and proof. It is true of course that interpolation is a valid procedure but we must be cautious when we extrapolate. Actually it is this procedure which is followed by those who would assume uniformitarianism in dating by radioactive decay. They are extrapolating the rate of radioactive decay back into the past. Experiences which we have had in extrapolating from animal results to human results should teach us to be very cautious. Deductions which are reached by extrapolation deserve to be taken with a grain of salt. Extrapolation is valid in suggesting lines of study and experimentation and in suggesting cause and effect relationships. However, extrapolation is not valid as a proof.

It is clear that much of the structure of modern evolutionary paleontology rests upon assumptions which are by their very nature not capable of verification. Many of these are quite logical and at present appear to be preferable to other alternatives that have been proposed by science. Many of them are also fruitful in scientific studies. But we should recognize that they are assumptions and that as such they are not capable of proof. We should also recognize that still more logical and fruitful assumptions may develop in the course of scientific studies. The observations which we make in science do not change, but the explanations may. There is no disagreement with many of the observations of paleontology, but there may be disagreement with the interpretations which are placed on these observations.

Notes

1. William S. Beck, *Modern Science and the Nature of Life* (New York: Harcourt, Brace, 1957), p. 170.
2. Maurice Caullery, *Les Etapes de la Biologie* (Paris: University of France, 1941), p. 125.
3. G. A. Kerkut, *Implications of Evolution* (New York: Pergamon, 1960), p. 150–57.
4. G. Bonnier, quoted in W. B. Turrill, *Experimental and Synthetic Plant Taxonomy in the New Systematics,* Julian Huxley, ed. (Oxford: Oxford University Press, 1940), p. 55 ff.
5. Frederic E. Clements, Emmett V. Martin and Frances L. Long, *Adaptation and Origin in the Plant World* (Waltham, Mass.: Chronica Botanica, 1950), p. 173.
6. Th. Dobzhansky, *Genetics and the Origin of Species* (New York: Columbia University, 1951), p. 257.
7. Kerkut, loc. cit.
8. Edwin H. Colbert, *Dinosaurs* (New York: Dutton, 1961), p. 146 f.
9. Edwin H. Colbert, *The Dinosaur Book* (New York: McGraw-Hill, 1951), p. 55.
   William King Gregory, *Evolution Emerging* (New York: Macmillan, 1951), I, 327.
10. Earnest Albert Hooton, *Up from the Ape* (New York: Macmillan, 1946), p. 329.
11. George Gaylord Simpson, *Some Principles of Historical Biology Bearing on Human Origins* (Cold Spring Harbor Symposia on Quantitative Biology, 15 [1950]), p. 57 ff.

3 • Uniformity, Uniformitarianism, and the Foundations of Science

Kenneth L. Currie

The object of science is the acquisition and organization of empirical knowledge; that is, the investigation of phenomena not dependent on the subjective state of the investigator. One might suppose that all aspects of reality are colored by the will. This view has been discredited by the impressive growth of science and its more materialistic offshoot, technology. This success however does not validate the basic assumption of science, that there is a basic construct, which may be called a "fact" totally independent of subjective influence. This assumption must be accepted or rejected on grounds outside the body of science.

If it be allowed that facts can be discerned, then sense observations may be collected and catalogued, including the results obtained from extensions of our senses, that is, dials, gauges, and so forth. To protect themselves against frauds of evil intent, or merely of enthusiasm, scientists have formulated two tests which must be passed before an observation can be considered a fact. First, it must be repeatable, that is, the same concatenation of circumstances always produces the same result. Second, it must be impersonal, that is, the same set of circumstances yields the same observation to different observers or to a suitably adjusted machine. These two simple rules have been of great utility in building up the corpus of fact upon which science and technology is based. However, the price has been high. Science has necessarily rejected as meaningless all knowledge which is singular and personal, thus giving up the areas of knowledge which may well be most critical for human welfare.

From the vast array of observed facts we may pick out subsets which possess in common certain arbitrarily chosen qualities. From this subset we may construct the basic unit of scientific reasoning, the correlation. A correlation assumes that a certain concatenation of observables has a unique physical significance. For example we observe that all objects within the influence of the earth's gravitational field fall toward the center of the earth. We *assume* that this common property has physical significance, and use it to define the concept of gravitational field. It is possible, however, that each object that falls toward the center of the earth does so for a separate and distinct reason not connected with gravitation. If we assume that *some* concatenation of observables has unique significance, then we may use statistical means to show that the existence of the gravitational field is so overwhelmingly probable as to be a practical certainty. The assumption that a complex and often repeated sequence of events is not fortuitous, but reflects an underlying regularity may be termed the uniformity principle.

The formation of a correlation is one of the many points in science at which personality enters. The same data may well yield nothing to one investigator, yet another may discover a fruitful and significant result. A correlation may in itself be a significant result, or it may be the foundation for an exercise in induction. For example, if a scientist were to formulate the correlation, "All people who contract cancer have blue eyes," or even "Seven out of 10 people who contract cancer have blue eyes," this would be a sensational result, and a great deal of further effort would certainly go into verifying the statistics involved. However, tautologous correlations, or those which belabor the obvious have no value unless they can be used as the foundation for a further advance. It must be noted that any correlation is of a statistical character. While a correlation may be destroyed by the accumulation of more observational data, it cannot be rendered mathematically certain by such accumulation. There is always a finite possibility that a further observation may disprove the correlation. After the application of suitable statistical methods, we may say that this possibility is extremely small, but not that it is impossible.

Correlations alone do not enlighten us about the underlying regularities assumed to exist by the principle of uniformity. However, the existence of strong correlations tends to reinforce our belief that such regularities do exist. In order to discover information about the processes producing the correlations, it is necessary to reason from models. A model is a construction in thought (or reality) of a portion of the universe with all extraneous elements removed. In this simplified area the interactions of the remaining elements may be closely observed. The usefulness of the model depends on how closely it simulates real conditions and how wide a range of phenomena it is able to explain. Obviously models are subject to a great deal of refinement if the effort is considered worthwhile. Scientific "knowledge" today consists of a large number of models of various aspects of the universe. In one discipline the models tend to be quite similar, or at least noncontradictory, but considering the whole breadth of science there are numerous models in common use which are mutually contradictory. There is general agreement that these models could be brought into harmony if there were sufficient observational data, and deep enough insight into this data. According to this assumption, the large number of theories and principles underlying the various models could be reduced to a very few, or possibly a single all-embracing principle. It is generally supposed that these basic truths could be expressed in a simple manner. Many scientists feel that this is their search for God. This simplicity principle is the philosophical foundation of science and scientists who make a contribution toward the realization of this principle, such as Albert Einstein, are considered the great men of science.

It is necessary to have some ground rules for the construction of models. By general agreement no model can be considered valid until an actual example of the proposed mechanism can be demonstrated. This basic rule constitutes the actuality principle, and motivates experimental and observational science. Note that the failure of a scientific theory does not necessarily imply that the supposed process does not work, nor that the observations were wrong, nor even that the correlation was faulty, but simply that the model was defective. This point is often misunderstood by nonscientists who suppose that the failure of a theory undermines the scientific method in general, and casts into doubt large bodies of scientific knowledge. In fact the reverse is true. Scientists work within the confines of their models. The well-understood areas of knowledge are satisfactorily explained by the model, and it suggests experiments on the boundaries of knowledge. Models, particularly old ones, tend to become very cramping in that they eventually lose logical fertility, that is they suggest no new lines of research. Hence the collapse or replacement of a model tends to suddenly open out a field of research not seen before because of preoccupation with the model. It is no accident that scientific revolutions such as relativity, quantum mechanics, the destruction of parity, are followed by outbursts of scientific creativity.

Thus far we have been speaking about the ideal development of science. In practice matters turn out somewhat differently, particularly in the early development of a discipline. Every discipline discovers rather early a few major guiding principles. In physics these were the conservation of energy, mass, and momentum; in chemistry the discreteness and immutability of elements; in geology the maxim "The present is the key to the past." These principles are then enshrined as inviolate, and further progress is based upon them. The particular discipline may then be called "uniformitarian," in analogy with the geological doctrine of uniformitarianism enunciated by Charles Lyell. This uniformitarian phase is one of rapid progress, when the basic framework of the discipline is established. Presently however it becomes apparent that certain observations stubbornly refuse to be reconciled with the guiding principle. More or less satisfactory patchwork compromises are made until a genius such as Copernicus, or Einstein, or Pasteur suddenly sees that the guiding principle can be abandoned, and its essential content saved in a much broader and less rigid frame. The science is then freed to develop in a more natural and unhampered manner. As a general rule the name of the old principle is retained and honored, though the spirit is totally altered. Thus physics still has a principle of conservation of mass and energy—though totally different from the original. Chemistry still pays lip service to the idea of conservation of elements, and many geologists claim to be uniformitarian, even while proposing unidirectional evolution of the earth.

This ambivalence confuses many laymen, who suppose scientists would adhere to obsolete and discredited theories. It does have a value however in immortalizing the name of scientific innovators. We remember Newton not for the invention of calculus, or his *Principia Mathematica,* because these achievements are easily within the reach of any college student today, but for Newtonian gravitation, the theory of which was perfected by Laplace 150 years after Newton. We remember scientists not so much for what they actually did but for the potential that was in their work.

Consider the status and development of the geologic sciences. Geology has never suffered from any lack of observational facts. Rather it has been retarded by the disproportionately large amount of data to be hung on a meager theoretical frame. There is no lack of correlations of geological facts. However, here the difficulties begin to appear. In any large body of data 'pseudo-correlations' begin to appear, and in any group of data involving a large number of variables it may be difficult to determine the cause and effect relationships from merely covariant results. Many geological models have been proposed. The basis on which these models have been constructed vary, but there are at least three distinct varieties: (1) those based on an observed analogue, (2) those based on an extrapolated analogue, (3) those based on scale model experiments.

Obviously it would be desirable to have all geological reasoning based on the first type of model, but there are two difficulties: spatial and temporal. These difficulties are particularly obvious in discussions of the formation of large geological structures, such as mountain ranges. For example, geological mapping in some mountain areas suggests that vast plates of rock hundreds of square miles in area and a few hundred or thousand feet in thickness have slid tens of miles. Small plates of rock up to a few hundred feet in diameter can be observed to slide over their surroundings. From this observation one might *extrapolate* to suppose that much larger masses could do the same thing.

Such extrapolations must be received with caution, because experience has shown that very large masses are often qualitatively as well as quantitatively different from small ones. Even if the large mass would slide in the short term, it is by no means obvious that it would slide over geological time, because rock properties often show unexpected (and unknown) time dependence over long periods. In cases where neither observation nor extrapolation are practicable, it may be possible to build a scale model which will compress both space and time. Difficulties in this undertaking are formidable. For example, if the earth were reduced to a sphere three feet in diameter, it should be modelled in part from material with the consistency of thin mud. Obviously this is impossible since a model of this composition will not hold a spherical shape. Model experiments are therefore regarded with some mistrust. Nevertheless theories based on the second or third type of evidence may at any moment become based on the first and most powerful type of evidence. For example, the idea that turbidity currents transport large amounts of material on the ocean floor and cause erosion has been current for a century and was experimentally demonstrated by Kuenen in 1940. Ewing and Heezen showed in 1959, from their analysis of the Grand Banks earthquake of 1929, that a turbidity current had in fact resulted from this tremor.

Extrapolated and laboratory evidence is gradually gaining greater acceptance in geologic thinking. A basic problem is the proper handling of geologic time. If one accepts the evidence that geologic time has extended over thousands of millions of years, it is manifest that proper extrapolations cannot be made over this period from contemporary evidence. Similarly even well-conceived and executed modelling experiments may fail to show suitable temporal effects. However, we must remember that physical science is all one. Einstein's greatest achievement was to show that the nature of space is intimately connected with physical events, and that time is inextricably related to space. The relation of space and time is thus turned into a kind of ergodic problem, the demonstration of the equivalence of certain spatial ensembles with certain temporal ensembles. Although this problem has not been solved, great progress has been made by Khinchin, Birkhoff, and others, and it is known that such equivalences exist. There is no observational evidence whatever for assuming that space-time relations were essentially different in the past, and there is strong, though indirect, evidence that they were not.

In common with other scientists geologists can collect verifiable, observational data, arrange such data into meaningful sequences, obtain experimental corroboration of critical points, and construct models with logical consequences. Insofar as these models extrapolate into the past or predict into the future, these predictions have the same kind of validity as any other scientific prediction. Of course every science is concerned with particular aspects of empirical reality. In geology time is of more consequence than it is in some other disciplines, but quantitative variations cannot obscure the fundamental unity of science.

The history of geology yields a fascinating insight into the origin of modern ideas. The change from deduction to induction is perhaps nowhere better exemplified. Abraham G. Werner (1750–1817) lectured at the Freiburg Mining Academy for 40 years and was the most influential geologist of his age. Werner emphasized the great importance of sedimentary successions, although he was not the first to realize that such successions exist. Werner was aware that the character of the earth's surface had evolved over time, but from his researches in the Erzgebirge he concluded that *all* the rocks, including the crystalline basement had been deposited from an all-encompassing sea. This sea had gradually subsided, depositing sediments continuously, and its remnants were still doing so.

Werner's theory had fatal defects which are extremely instructive. First, where did the excess water go when the ocean drained? It was quite obvious even in Werner's time that it could not disappear into the earth. Werner himself thought perhaps it had disappeared into outer space, but never made any definite commitment. In any case it was obvious that appeal to a singular, nonreproducible mechanism had to be made. This was fatal. Second, the "primitive" rocks and basalts were soon shown to result from igneous action. It was on this point that the "Neptunian" theory really suffered wreck. The production of numerous contemporary examples of supposedly "Neptunian" rocks resulting from igneous processes discredited the theory. Third, areas were found where sedimentary sequences were tens of times as thick as they were in other places. This was very difficult to understand if the ocean had been universal. In brief, the Neptunian theory wrecked because (1) it did not use scientific principles for interpretation of observational data, (2) it failed to demonstrate the possibility of its assumed mechanism (actuality principle), and (3) it was based on too narrow a selection of data.

The great opponent of Werner's Neptunian theory was James Hutton, (1726–1797). Unlike Werner whose work was virtually confined to the Erzgebirge, Hutton had travelled widely, and had correspondents all over the world. He did not attempt to force his data into a preconceived mold, but applied only logical rules. Hutton made two basic discoveries. First, in many places the sedimentary strata had been tipped up from their original horizontal position to steep angles, bevelled off, and new horizontal strata deposited on top of them. In some places this process had occurred many successive times. Second, the tilted rocks had been forceably intruded by crystalline rocks, usually of granitic type. The series of rocks thus contorted and penetrated by plutonic material had at a later time been wasted away by the destructive action of the atmosphere, thus acquiring a more or less level surface on which new deposits, often consisting of the debris of the old, were laid down. Each of these "unconformities" marks a revolution, and evidences of successive revolutions are found throughout the geologic column.

In contemplating the history of the earth, to use the famous dictum of Hutton, "We find no sign of a beginning—no prospect of an end." Hutton's arguments were—and are—so conclusive and so obvious that within 30 years every eminent geologist had abandoned the Neptunian theory, and no theory of geology supposing the earth's surface to result completely, or mainly, from receding waters has ever since been able to attract a single outstanding geologist.

Practically contemporaneous with Hutton, Baron Georges

Cuvier (1769–1818) was establishing the science of paleontology. For a century fossils had been generally recognized as lithified remains of once living organisms. The great achievement of Cuvier, an outstanding biologist, was the demonstration that skeletons, and even partial skeletons could be made to yield useful information about the long-dead animals. He was able to show that most of the fossils, though distantly related to living species, were separate and extinct species. Cuvier also seems to have recognized that the fossil content of a stratum was a distinguishing characteristic. Cuvier thought that between each series of strata with a different fossil fauna, a "catastrophe" must have occurred, such that all animals were killed, and a new creation had occurred to people each succeeding sequence. This conception would seem to draw something from Hutton's idea of "revolutions," but I have been unable to discover whether Cuvier in fact drew on Hutton's work.

Paleontology was welded onto geology by the great English geologist, William Smith (1769–1839). Smith was primarily a surveyor and engineer, and his geological work began as a utilitarian project. He was chiefly interested in establishing routes for canals and in mapping coalfields. In the course of this work he noticed that certain characteristic beds could be followed for many miles, and that each of these beds was characterized by a unique fossil content (a possibility pointed out 100 years earlier by Robert Hooke). As a result of more than 20 years of travel and observation he published a geological map of England, with the strata characterized by their fossil content. It would not be too much to say that Smith established geology as a profession, and founded the art of stratigraphy. In his map of England, Smith noted, as did Hutton, that there were certain natural divisions in the strata, marked by structural peculiarities, that is, unconformities. Smith termed each of these divisions "systems." The end of each system was marked by a revolution, during which the strata were folded and generally upheaved and deformed.

When Smith's work became famous, evidence of these revolutions was searched for elsewhere. This was done with outstanding success in western Europe, but as the extensions reached further and further, the scheme was found to be less satisfactory. While revolutions occurred in every sequence, they were not everywhere contemporaneous. Indeed it was found that no revolution had a worldwide or even continentwide significance. Cuvier's catastrophic theory foundered on this basic observational fact, just as the diluvial theory foundered on the fact that there were revolutions in every geological sequence. The geologic column could not be explained by assuming either a singular short-lived process, or by a sequence of static episodes separated by universal catastrophes. To paraphrase a famous theological aphorism, nature could be interpreted only by nature.

This fundamental tenet of science was hammered in by Charles Lyell. Lyell was not a profound original thinker, but he had great organizing ability and great influence, both scientific and social. Lyell welded into a system the work of the English stratigraphers. He was so impressed by the failure of preconceived notions, that he went to the opposite extreme of claiming that only processes now operating were of any geologic significance. He also suggested that these processes had always operated at about the same rate as they do now, although he wavered alarmingly about this point. These theses constituted the theory of uniformitariansim. Lyell failed to see that his work contained exactly the same flaw as that of the catastrophists, namely a presupposition not supported by the geologic record. However, his work contained the corrective measures necessary to remove this flaw: the insistence that *all* the evidence be considered and the wholesale reliance on the actuality principle. It is because of these latter circumstances that Lyell is entitled to be called the father of scientific geology. Although his own work was flawed, it contained the potential of a more perfect sequel. Lyell was honest enough to live by the principles he enunciated. Although he was a strong opponent of the Darwinian theory of evolution, he eventually convinced himself that the evidence in its favor was incontrovertible, and publicly declared himself converted.

Lyell's error was that he sought to make an inductive science yield deductively certain conclusions. His more perceptive contemporaries rightly saw that this was impossible. The best that was possible was the formulation of a probable conclusion. The probability might be extremely high, but the conclusion was not a certainty. There was a curious bias in 19th-century thinking against "almost universal" results, which seems to have been connected with the widespread prevalence of optimistic materialism.

This capsule review of geological thought may be concluded with a note on the great petrologist N. L. Bowen. Lyell had shown that geology could be treated like any other physical science. Bowen firmly welded it onto the other sciences. Geological experiments had been attempted before Bowen, and his own work was based on that of Vogt and Rosenbusch, but he was the first to insist that experiment and field evidence could be correlated. An excellent field geologist, as well as a great physical chemist, he was the first to take results from the laboratory to the field instead of vice versa. Bowen also exerted a powerful influence on the tendency to present results statistically—in accordance with the fundamental limitations of science.

In a little less than 200 years, therefore, we can observe the progress of geological science from nonsensory deductions to statistically based conclusions from observations. The former were alleged to yield "true" results, the latter only probable results. The conceptual frame of geology is firmly established, and by close adherence to the actuality principle we can be assured that it will not shift very greatly. Nevertheless any geological conclusion is subject to alteration. This is an immutable law of science, if such a thing exists. This alteration however will not affect the observational evidence, nor the correlations between evidence. We cannot rely on scientific progress to obliterate facts which we may find distasteful.

To summarize, we conclude that the foundations of science rest upon three assumptions—entirely independent of methodological considerations or the demands of a particular discipline. These may be paraphrased as follows: (1) There exist nontrivial, measurable data not subject to the subjective state of the investigator (zeroth principle). (2) Interactions between these data (though not the data themselves) show a high degree of regularity (uniformity principle). (3) The regularities can be described in comprehensible and manipulable form (simplicity principle). In addition to these basic considerations, present methods of investigation assume that (4) interactions or processes occurring in models of physical reality can be demonstrated by experiment (actuality principle).

Section II

Time in Scripture and Geology

A Statement of the Problem

PAUL A. ZIMMERMAN

This section explores two aspects of the question of the age of the earth. The chapter on Ussher's chronology examines the validity of using the genealogies of the Bible as chronologies. It seeks to determine if the Bible itself provides a date for the act of creation.

The second chapter in this section looks at the age of the earth from the viewpoint of the geologist. What is the history of geological dating? What are the most accurate methods of determining the age of the rocks? What are the fundamental assumptions made by scientists as they apply research to the question of the age of our planet? It must be remembered that no chain of scientific thought is any stronger than the links of the assumptions that help to make up that chain. Subject to the limitation of these assumptions, what is the composite picture of the earth's age as determined by various methods?

Thus the reader may gain an appreciation of the approach both of the theologian and of the practicing geologist. It is obvious from the material here presented that the question is complex. But it must be emphasized that this chapter by no means endeavors to explore all aspects of the date of the beginning. For example, the length of the creation day is not treated. The nature of time itself is not explored.

Also unexplored in this section are the disputed translations of Gen. 1:1-2, which have achieved prominence in recent years. Two translations of the Hebrew text seem possible. The common and more generally accepted is that of the Revised Standard Version: "In the beginning God created the heavens and the earth. The earth was without form and void, and darkness was upon the face of the deep; and the Spirit of God was moving over the face of the waters. . . ."

A different rendering is represented by the 1962 translation of the Jewish Publication Society of America, known as *The Torah:* "When God began to create the heaven and the earth—the earth being unformed and void, with darkness over the surface of the deep and a wind (Spirit) from God sweeping over the water . . . ."

Both translations appear to be possible on the basis of grammar. Competent students of the Old Testament, including Jewish scholars, may be found on both sides of the syntactical argument. However, the conventional translation of the Revised Standard Version seems to be more generally accepted.

The translation of the Jewish Publication Society makes possible the interpretation that Genesis is telling us of the creation of the earth, with nothing being said as to the creation of matter or possibly the universe itself. This in turn opens the door to speculation concerning what had happened prior to the Genesis account. There is no question that the Holy Scriptures credit God with all creative activity. But, some wonder, was there a universe and an earth before the events recorded in Genesis 1?

Some see evidence of an earlier world in passages such as: Is. 45:18, Jer. 4:23-26, and Ezek. 28:11-19. There are several variations of this idea. They are commonly known as "gap theories" or restoration theories. They usually postulate the fall of the evil angels and subsequent destruction, followed by a new creation.

Suffice it to say in this brief treatment that the passages in Jeremiah, Ezekiel, and Isaiah do not appear to support the gap theory. But it seems wise to note that some feel that it is legitimate to translate Gen. 1:1-2 in a manner which would make it clear that much time could have elapsed before the beginning of a six-day creative activity. Others believe that much time may have been involved in the Spirit of God moving over the face of the waters.

Variables such as these make it quite impossible to be dogmatic theologically concerning the age of the earth. Nor is it possible for the scientist in turn to be dogmatic. He too is confronted with many variables as well as the limits of his assumptions. In this connection see the discussion of Dr. John Klotz in his chapter on the role of assumptions in scientific thought.

It should also be clearly recognized that the question of the age of the earth and of evolution are separate questions. An ancient earth in itself does not provide proof for evolution. It is true, of course, that the evolutionist requires billions of years for life to evolve and develop. But the creationist does not base his doctrine on the question of time. When did God carry out His great creative acts? How long has man been on the earth? These are questions quite independent of the basic question of the origin of life and in particular of the historicity of Adam and Eve.

It is true that a postulated great antiquity for man troubles some. But is not the reason for this to be found in preconceived notions? Some ask: Through how many generations could God preserve the covenant He made with man without the truth being lost? Some impose a definite limit. But this too is speculation. God's power and grace are without limit. This in the final analysis is the main point.

4 • A Critical Evaluation of the Chronology of Ussher

Fred Kramer

A popular college textbook in historical geology makes the statement that Archbishop Ussher of Ireland, "In 1654 deduced from his study of the Scriptures that the Creation had taken place on the 26th of October in the year 4004, B. C., at nine o'clock in the morning." He adds, "Unfortunately, this very specific date was inserted by some unknown authority as a marginal reference in the King James Version of the Bible, and thus became implanted in religious creed." [1]

The author of this textbook states on page 29 that from the calculations of geologists, according to the so-called atomic clock, "It is clear that the earth is more than two billion years old." Since that time geologists have revised their estimates upward, so that the age of the earth is today more often quoted in terms of 4½ to 5 billion years.

It should be said here that Archbishop Ussher was not the only one who sought to establish a chronology which would permit him to set the date, not only of such important events as the Noachian Flood, the Tower of Babel, and the birth of Abraham, but of the very creation of the earth itself. Even before Archbishop Ussher, the Lutheran Calvisius had made similar calculations which were in use for a long time in Lutheran circles. Abraham Calov, in his *Systema Locorum Theologicorum,* places the Exodus, according to the chronology of Calvisius, in the year 2453, after the creation of the world.[2] Ussher places it in the year 2513, leaving the two celebrated chronologists 60 years apart on this date. Martin Luther had made similar calculations when he delivered his famous lectures on the Book of Genesis, as is evident from the fact that he has the patriarch Eber outliving Abraham by 64 years.[3]

Likewise, Luther has Noah living well into the age of Abraham, and assumes that Noah was Abraham's teacher.[4] Luther assumes, on the basis of similar calculations, that the famed Melchisedec is identical with Shem, the son of Noah.[5]

The Christian who is nurtured on the King James Version of the Bible and has the figures from the chronology of Ussher in his Bible is likely to be greatly disturbed by the great number of years for the age of the universe assumed by scientists today.

It is not our purpose at this point to examine the validity of the calculations of the scientists. This can and must be done by scientists employing the scientific method. Our purpose here is to examine the validity of the method employed by Ussher and other theologians of bygone generations to establish the age of the earth and the date of the Flood, the Tower of Babel, and the patriarch Abraham. The method employed by Ussher and others who constructed chronologies was to take the genealogical tables in Scriptures, particularly in Genesis, chapters 5 and 11, where there are lists of patriarchs. These lists give their names, the age at which they fathered descendants, and their age at the time of their death. By a system of calculations based on these figures Ussher arrived at the date of 4004 B. C. for the time of the creation of the world; 2349 for the date of the Flood; 2247 for the Tower of Babel; 1921 for Abraham. Other chronologists, using the same method as that pursued by Ussher, arrive at slightly different results. However, their findings are comparable in general.

We propose to show in the following that Scripture itself discredits the use of genealogies for the purpose of establishing a precise chronology for the age of the earth, the dates of the patriarchs, the Flood, Abraham, and any of the events connected with the times before Abraham.

We propose not to begin with the genealogical tables in Genesis 5 and 11, but near the end of the New Testament, and to work backward. In this way we shall see how the holy writers deal with matters of genealogy, and will then be able to evaluate the method used by Ussher and his contemporaries.

The first passage to note is Hebrews 7:9, 10 which says: "Levi also, who receiveth tithes, payed tithes in Abraham. For he was yet in the loins of his father, when Melchisedec met him" (KJV). The Bible reader of the 20th century is at first nonplussed to read that Levi was in the loins of Abraham. Levi, as we understand relationships and chronology, was not a son of Abraham but rather the patriarch's great-grandson, Isaac and Jacob being generations between Levi and Abraham. Abraham himself was 100 years old when his son Isaac was born (Gen. 21:5). Isaac was more than 40 years old when his son Jacob was born (Gen. 25:20-21). Jacob was far more than 40 years old when Levi was born (Gen. 26:34; 29:18, 31-34). The whole age of Abraham was only 175 years (Gen. 25:7-8). It was evident from all this that Abraham was long dead when Levi was born. Yet the writer to the Hebrews says that Levi was in the loins of his father, namely Abraham, when Melchisedec met him.

One must not, however, imagine for one moment that the writer to the Hebrews had a lapse of memory. Without doubt he knew very well what he was doing. He was simply doing what was common in Jewish circles in his time. Any ancestor was regarded as the father of all his descendants—no matter how many generations the descendants were removed. This is evident even to the casual reader of the New Testament in Matt. 1:1: "The book of the generation of Jesus Christ, the son of David, the son of Abraham." The very verses that follow show that there are a number of generations between Christ and David and again also between David and Abraham. (Matt. 1:2-16)

Even genealogies which, to judge from the manner in which they are set forth, would appear to be exact also by Western standards, are often not so. Individual generations, at times a fairly large number of generations, are intentionally and knowingly omitted without a shadow of suspicion that either an error or a fraud is committed thereby.

The genealogy which follows Matt. 1:2-17 is a good example. In verses 2-6, Matthew lists the generations from Abraham to David; in verses 6-11, the generations between David and the Babylonian Captivity; and in verses 12-17, the generations between the Babylonian Captivity and the birth of Jesus. In verse 17 the evangelist sums up as follows: "So *all* the generations from Abraham to David are fourteen generations; and from David until the carrying away into Babylon are fourteen generations; and from the carrying away into Babylon unto Christ are fourteen generations."

Matthew appears to be presenting a very exact genealogy. Yet when we examine the records in the Old Testament, we find that Matthew omits generations at two points. In verse 8 the evangelist informs us: "And Joram begat Ozias." Ozias is the Septuagint form of Uzziah. When we examine the genealogy in the Old Testament on which Matthew's genealogy is based, we find that Matthew omits three generations, namely Ahaziah, Joash, and Amaziah (cf. 2 Kings 8:25; 11:2; 14:1). Farther down in his genealogy, in verse 11, Matthew lists Josias as begetting Jechonias. However, the Old Testament in 2 Kings 23:34, and 1 Chron. 3:16 informs us that Jehoiakim was the son of Josias, and the father of Jechonias. Thus Matthew has omitted one more generation.

An interesting case of the same kind is found in 1 Chron. 23:15-16 and 1 Chron. 26:24 where the genealogy Moses, Gershom, and Shebuel is found. Moses is too well known to need comment. Shebuel was one of the officers of King David. The time between Moses and David covers a period of more than 400 years. It is unthinkable that there should have been only three generations during a 400-year period. It is evident that many generations have here been omitted, as appears to be customary in the genealogies of both the Old and of the New Testament.

Instructive also is the case of Jeriah, who was also one of the officers of King David. We read of him in 1 Chron. 26:31. Jeriah is said to be the son of Hebron (1 Chron. 23:19), who in turn was the son of Koath (1 Chron. 23:12), who was the son of Levi (1 Chron. 23:6). This takes us back not merely to the days of Moses and the Exodus, which would amount to about 480 years, but actually to the days before Israel went down into Egypt, an additional period of at least 430 years. Therefore a period of 900 years is covered by four generations. It should be evident that here many generations have been omitted in the genealogy.

The genealogy of the prophet and statesman Ezra is also instructive. This genealogy is given twice, namely, Ezra 7:1-5, and 1 Chron. 6:3-14, in which passage the genealogy is only carried to Seraiah, the father of Ezra. The 1 Chronicles passage has all the names found in the Ezra passage, but in addition has six names not found in Ezra. After the six that are omitted, later eight more follow which are precisely alike both in Ezra and in 1 Chronicles. One cannot but conclude that at least six generations are skipped in Ezra without any indication that this was done.

We have listed some of the examples of omitted generations in Biblical genealogies. Others could be cited.[6]

We are now ready to ask some questions with respect to the genealogies in Genesis 5 and Genesis 11, which above all others were used by Archbishop Ussher and his contemporaries to construct the type of chronology which led to the conclusion that the date of the creation of the world was about 4004 B. C. If, as is evident, the holy writers did not in many instances either attempt or claim to construct genealogies in which all generations were included, then we must assume that the writer of Genesis 5 and 11 may possibly have followed the same method. A number of generations, perhaps many generations, may have been omitted in these genealogies. The age which is given for the father at the birth of a given son tends to support the conclusion that there is an unbroken sequence. Yet it is possible that the purpose instead is to indicate the age of child production in those patriarchal times as well as the greater span of human life. Other generations may have come between the individuals named.

If this is the case, then the dates of Abraham, of the Tower of Babel, of the Flood, and of the Creation itself will be pushed farther into the past. Moreover, there are certain indications in the Scripture itself to the effect that also in these particular genealogies generations were omitted. Perhaps the most tangible evidence to this effect is found in the genealogy of Jesus in Luke 3:36, where Cainan is called the son of Arphaxad, and the father of Sala. In Gen. 11:12 Sala appears not as the grandson of Arphaxad, but as his son. The name of Cainan does not appear in the Massoretic text of Genesis 11.[7] It thus appears here from the New Testament that in Genesis 11 also at least one generation has been omitted.

Some students of the Holy Scripture have argued on other grounds that probably many generations have been omitted in the genealogies between the Flood and the Tower of Babel. They are struck by the fact that according to the chronology of Ussher, based on the genealogy in Genesis 11, the Tower of Babel was built 102 years after the end of the Deluge. They frankly doubt the correctness of this reckoning on two grounds. First of all, they doubt that in 102 years eight people would have multiplied to the point where a project like the Tower of Babel could have been undertaken. Second, they doubt that during the lifetime of Noah wickedness and idolatry would have gained so great a foothold that such a project would be undertaken.[8] These same authors argue in a somewhat similar manner for a longer time period between the Tower of Babel and Abraham.[9]

In addition to these arguments in favor of considering the genealogies in Genesis 5 and 11 to be abbreviated, Bible students have pointed to the fact that both of these genealogies list 10 generations, 10 from Adam to Noah, and 10 from Seth, the son of Noah, to Abraham. They point out that this suggests that the genealogies might have been brought to this even number artificially, as the genealogy of Christ in Matt. 1:1-17 was artificially made to conform to the 14-14-14 pattern. This argument, admittedly, is not conclusive. But the fact remains that the evidence points in this direction. Such a conclusion is in line with what the careful student can readily observe as he studies other genealogical tables in Scripture.

In our evaluation of the method of computing chronology on the basis of genealogy, as employed by Ussher and others, we have come to the conclusion that the method is wrong and unsupported by the Scripture itself. We cannot fail to note that the purpose of the genealogies in Scriptures is something far other than the computation of chronology. The Scripture is there because of Christ (Luke 24:44), and was written aforetime for our learning (Rom. 15:4), to make us wise unto salvation through faith which is in Christ Jesus (2 Tim. 3:15). The genealogies are there to enable the believer to know that Jesus, whom he accepts as his Lord and Savior, is actually, as was prophesied, the son of David, the son of Abraham. How many generations were omitted in drawing up these genealogies is of no importance for our real purpose, which is to testify to Christ and to the fulfillment of prophecy in Him. That many generations were omitted seems evident.

One question which we cannot refrain from asking here is: How much additional time may have elapsed between the time of the creation of the world and the Flood, between the Flood and the Tower of Babel, and between the Tower of Babel and Abraham, not indicated in the chronology of Ussher? On the one hand, this question cannot be avoided; on the other it cannot be answered with any degree of certainty. All that we can say with certainty is that the periods of time seem to be longer than calculated by Ussher, but we have no way of telling how much longer. Yet, good scholars have speculated here. There are those who feel that not more than a few thousand years, or at most a few tens of thousands of additional years can be gained. On the other hand there are others who believe that the periods of time in question may have been almost interminably long, running into hundreds of thousands, and perhaps even millions of years. A conservative estimate is that of John Klotz, who states:

> To the problem of the age of the earth Scripture gives us no definite answer. The figures of Bishop Ussher are not inspired, and his date for the Creation (4004 B. C.) does not appear to be correct. However, Scripture indicates that the age of the earth must be measured in thousands rather than millions and billions of years.[10]

The view of Henry M. Morris and John C. Whitcomb, Jr. is also conservative. These authors state:

> To stretch the genealogy of Genesis 11 to cover a period of over 100,000 years is to do violence to the chronological framework of all subsequent Bible history and prophecy. Approximately 2,000 years covers the history of the Church up to the present. Before Christ's first coming, the history of Israel covered a period of 2,000 years; and after Christ's second coming, according to Rev. 20, there will be another 1,000 years of earth-history before the commencement of the eternal state. (amillenialists do not even allow for these final 1,000 years). The incongruity of insisting upon 100,000 years between Noah and Abraham, while granting that the entire history of redemption from Abraham to the eternal state may be only four or five thousand years, becomes obvious.
>
> To be sure, it was by means of Biblical analogies that we were able to find possible gaps in the genealogy of Genesis 11. But the point we now wish to emphasize is that *those very analogies serve also to limit our time-scale for Genesis 11.* The gap between Amram and Moses was 300 years, not 30,000. And the gap between Joram and Oziah in Matt. 1:8 was 50 years, not 5,000. On the basis of the analogy of Biblical chronology, therefore, we maintain that it is very hazardous to assume a period of 100,000 years between the Flood and Abraham.[11]

Quite conservative also is the conclusion of this book. We quote:

> A careful study of the Biblical evidence leads us to the conclusion that the Flood may have occurred as much as three to five thousand years before Abraham. Some evangelical scholars, seeing the possibility of gaps in the genealogy of Genesis 11, have urged an acceptance of uniformitarian and evolutionary dating schemes for early man, with the Flood occurring more than 100,000 years ago. But the analogy of Biblical chronology. the obvious proximity of the judgment of

> Babel to the Flood, and the problem of Reu, Serug, and Nahor, make it highly improbable that such an extended postdiluvian chronology can be allowed. This improbability approaches impossibility when we consider the oral traditions of the Flood which have been incorporated into such documents as the Gilgamesh Epic of Babylonia.
>
> Evangelical scholars who feel the necessity of bringing Genesis 11 into conformity with current paleoanthropological time tables should realize the full implications of such harmonization efforts. It would seem to us that even the allowance of 5,000 years between the Flood and Abraham stretches Genesis 11 almost to the breaking point. The time has come when those who take the testimony of God's infallible Word with seriousness should begin to look with favor upon the efforts of those who are examining and exposing the unwarranted assumptions and false presuppositions of uniformitarianism as it applies to the dating of early man.[12]

Tending away from the conservative estimates of men like Klotz and Morris and Whitcomb, though still speaking discreetly, is this paragraph from Byron C. Nelson:

> The genealogies of Scripture must be regarded as abridged. God had no intention that they should be used for the construction of a chronology. So far as the Bible is concerned, the date of the creation of Adam and Eve may be many times earlier than Ussher supposed. While it is pure speculation at present to say that the human race is a hundred thousand years old, there is nothing in Scripture which forbids such an assumption. No proved or imagined antiquity of man can be too great to be accepted by Christians, since no fundamental doctrine is in any way involved.[13]

Even less conservative are the words of J. Oliver Buswell, Jr. This otherwise Biblical and conservative systematic theologian quotes Benjamin Warfield, a noted conservative theologian of a bygone generation:

As for the antiquity of man on the earth, we must bluntly say that the Bible gives us no data on which to base any conclusion, or even any estimate. Warfield, the greatest defender of the inerrancy of the Bible among scholarly theologians of the recent past, in discussing "The Antiquity and the Unity of the Human Race," says, ". . . for aught we know, instead of twenty generations and some two thousand years measuring the interval between the creation and the birth of Abraham, two hundred generations and something like twenty thousand years, or even two thousand generations and something like two hundred thousand years may have intervened. In a word, the scriptural data leave us wholly without guidance in estimating time which elapsed between the creation of the world and the deluge, and between the deluge and the call of Abraham. So far as the Scripture assertions are concerned, we may suppose any length of time to have intervened between these events which may otherwise appear reasonable."[14]

In summary, two things appear on the basis of our critical evaluation of the chronology of Ussher:

1. Ussher employed a method which is invalid and cannot but lead to invalid conclusions.
2. Scripture does not appear to be able to accommodate the billions of years demanded by uniformitarian scientists for the age of the earth.

Two recommendations are in order:

1. The chronology of Ussher should no longer be printed in the margin of English Bibles because it misleads rather than helps the reader.
2. Scientists who revere the Scripture and its teachings should continue to subject to careful scrutiny and criticism the time estimates of scientists who work in the framework of uniformitarianism.

Notes

1. Carl O. Dunbar, *Historical Geology* (New York: John Wiley and Sons, 1949), p. 21.
2. Abraham Calov, *Systema Locorum Theologicorum* (Wittenberg, 1655), p. 285.
3. *Luther's Works,* St. Louis Edition, Vol. 1, 716.
4. Ibid., p. 655.
5. Ibid., p. 898.
6. The interested reader should read Byron C. Nelson, *Before Abraham* (Minneapolis: Augsburg Publishing House, 1948), pp. 7–16.
7. It does appear in the text of the Septuagint, the Greek translation of the Old Testament. This raises questions not wholly germane to the present discussion. The Massoretic text may be defective at this point.
8. Henry M. Morris and John C. Whitcomb, Jr., *The Genesis Flood,* (Philadelphia: The Presbyterian and Reformed Publishing Co., 1962), p. 478.
9. Ibid., pp. 478, 479.
10. John W. Klotz, Ph. D., *Genes, Genesis and Evolution* (St. Louis: Concordia Publishing House, 1955), p. 116.
11. Morris and Whitcomb, pp. 485–86.
12. Ibid., p. 489.
13. Nelson, p. 16.
14. J. Oliver Buswell Jr., *A Systematic Theology of the Christian Religion* (Grand Rapids: Zondervan Publishing House, 1962), p. 325.

5 • Scientific Methods of Determining the Age of the Earth

Kenneth L. Currie

This chapter treats a subject in which there has been an explosive growth of knowledge in the past 30 years. Estimates of the age of the earth have passed from crude guesses toward highly sophisticated measurements. As a result of the vast increase in technical achievement, the principles underlying measurements have become more and more obscure. Readers untrained in the physical sciences may have the feeling of being hopelessly outdistanced by the mathematical and technical complexities of various methods of dating.

They should keep in mind that all methods of dating depend on the simple principle of the hourglass. We measure the amount of sand in the bottom (or the top) of the hourglass and tell how long it has been since the glass was last turned. The "sand" may be ever so complex, and the measurements of amounts superbly accurate, but the principle is unchanged. In the geological case, however, we must suppose that the hourglass may have a tiny leak through which sand slowly escapes, and that mischievous gremlins may occasionally give the glass a shake, or turn it over entirely. Finally, we are not quite certain of just how long it takes the sand to run through the glass. Such untoward events give rise to errors in telling time, whether present or geological. If the reader keeps these concepts in mind, the dating of geological events will lose much of its mystery.

Speculation on the age of the earth dates back almost as far as written records,[1] but modern scientific ideas on the subject are generally considered to stem from Steno (1638–1687) and Hooke (1635–1703). Thus computation of the age of the earth from observational data is a distinctively modern enterprise hardly more than 3 centuries old.

While Steno and Hooke were establishing the basis of historical geology, Biblical scholars were attempting to find the age of the earth by adding the ages of the patriarchs mentioned in the Old Testament. Calculations of this kind were made by Luther and others, but the chronology best known to English speaking peoples is that of Ussher (ca. 1654), which is often printed as a marginal gloss in the King James version of the Bible. Most of the chronologists obtained figures of about 6,000 years for the age of the earth, but discrepancies of several tens of years between various versions showed that there were difficulties. Leaving aside such exegetical hypotheses as the "gap theory," which denies the possibility of such calculations, Kramer has shown earlier in this section that the basic assumption of the chronologists was false. The genealogies of the Bible were not usually intended to serve as chronologies. Therefore chronologies based on these genealogies cannot be correct.

While Ussher was working on his chronology, the gradual recognition among scholars of the principle of uniformity was silently revolutionizing the study of the earth. As early as 1668 Hooke, in his *Discourse on Earthquakes*[2] had recognized the elements of the geostrophic cycle, the principle of unconformities, and the possibility of using fossils for stratigraphic dating. These ideas required more than 100 years to ripen, but throughout the 18th century the conviction gradually spread that land and water had changed places many times, that the Noachian flood was far too short to account for all fossiliferous strata, and that consequently the earth must be very old. Throughout the 18th century these views existed in tacit truce with the idea that the earth was about 6,000 years old.

The explosive growth of geological knowledge at the beginning of the 19th century pushed the vexing question of the age of the earth to the forefront. Charles Lyell, building on the work of Hutton, Werner, and William Smith, showed that many features of the earth's surface could be explained by the long-continued action of forces presently at work.[3] He presented evidence that these forces had acted on old rocks also. This view required enormous periods of time for the development of the present form of the earth, and was vigorously attacked by proponents of a 6,000-year age for the earth. The scientific evidence offered by the latter however was weak, and they were soon reduced to such reasoning as "The earth *appears* to be very old, but in fact is only 6,000 years old." Such propositions attracted little support. Proponents of a great age apparently had the evidence in their favor but had no concrete figure to offer. A clock was required.

A century of experience and experiment has shown that the selection and calibration of a geological clock is a task full of difficulty and hidden pitfalls. Natural processes in general do not act at fixed rates. The assumption that an average rate taken over a long period of time can be extrapolated is generally unsatisfactory. Although a number of geological clocks were tried during the century after Lyell's first publication of the *Principles of Geology,* it was clear to all scientists that the age of the earth was not known with any accuracy. However, the fact that all of the crude methods seemed to give ages of many millions of years gradually caused an acceptance of the view that the earth was very old. Keeping in mind that these methods are now known to be inaccurate, and are generally obsolete, we will consider some early scientific estimates of the age of the earth.

Lyell studied the changes in the structure of the shell of certain clams during the Tertiary period (geological periods referred to are shown in Appendix I, Table 1), and compared them with changes since the beginning of the ice age (Pleistocene).[4] He assumed the figure of 1 million years for the length of the Pleistocene and concluded that the Tertiary period covered about 80 million years. Radioactive methods today suggest duration of about 70 million years for the Tertiary period. Matthew[5] considered the evolution of the horse during the Tertiary period, compared to that in the Pleistocene, and obtained 60 million years for the length of the Tertiary. Note that the figures in both cases depend on the length of the Pleistocene. Since this unit is multiplied by 60 to 80, any initial error is multiplied accordingly. There are severe difficulties in this method relating to the definition of change in a fossil and time averaging of the change. While the quoted examples suggest an age of many millions of years for the earth, the numbers obtained are certainly unreliable.

Dana calculated the total thickness of sedimentary rocks laid down during Cenozoic, Mesozoic, and Paleozoic time, and obtained a ratio of 1:3:12.[6] Walcott corrected the ratio to 2:5:12,[7] which is generally accepted today. Using the best value of 68 million years for the Cenozoic this yields 645 million years for the Phanerozoic (the time since the beginning of the Cambrian). This figure is in reasonable agreement with radioactive measurement. Neither Dana nor Walcott came close to this figure. Dana used an obsolete estimate of the age of the earth by Lord Kelvin, and obtained only 36 million years. Walcott assumed a grossly excessive sedimentation rate of one foot per 200 years, and obtained 27.5 million years. Their contemporaries Reade[8] and Goodchild[9] used a more reasonable sedimentation rate and obtained answers of 600 to 700 million years.

The sedimentation method of age determination is suspect because it assumes: (a) the total thickness of rocks formed during a period of time is somewhere preserved; (b) the thickness of sedimentary rock is proportional to the time required for its formation; and (c) sedimentation rate, a notoriously erratic process, has a meaningful average value over millions of years.[10] Despite these difficulties, the method has been revived by Schuchert.[11] By means of radioactive dating Holmes has shown that the rate of sedimentation averaged over millions of years has been remarkably constant since the Precambrian.[12] This is a justification of the sediment method. Sonder has elaborated a science for finding the time taken for deposition of sedimentary beds, taking into account their chemistry, lithology, and tectonic setting.[13] While less satisfactory than radioactive dating, this type of scheme can probably be made to yield results within 25 to 50 percent of the correct value.

Both of the foregoing methods depend on the length of the Pleistocene (the time of ice ages). This period, which merges imperceptibly with the present, can be dated by (a) tree rings, (b) varves, and (c) astronomical cycles. In temperate climates trees usually add one ring to their growth in a year. Hence by taking a cross section of the trunk we may count up the annual rings and find the age of the tree. However, all of these rings are not identical. Their thickness and character may vary depending on climatic and other conditions. Hence it is possible to correlate distinctive rings from one tree to another.[14] By comparing sufficient numbers of trees, beams, logs and so forth, a chronology may be built up extending back about 6,000 years. This is entirely within the historical period in many areas, so that conclusions about climate and cycles can be checked.

The varve method is essentially similar. Varves are fine beds of clay or silt which commonly form annually in some glacier-fed lakes. The character of the varve varies with climatic and other conditions, and hence can be traced from place to place. Varves are presently forming along the Angerman River in northern Sweden, and this deposit is used to define the zero in time.[15] DeGeer,[16] Sauramo,[17] and others have extended the chronology back about 13,500 years in Scandinavia with a discrepancy between Sweden and Finland of about 54 years. More controversial counts have been made in North America by Antevs,[18] extending back about 18,000 years. Varves are most helpful in establishing weather and astronomical cycles of more than one year. Varves are not helpful in attempting to establish worldwide, rather than local, time scales, and attempts to do so must be regarded with suspicion. In addition, laminations of shorter time period may locally obscure true annual varves. Study of varve-type sediments is not restricted to either Pleistocene glacial material, or to recent sediments. Korn[19] counted varves in the Carboniferous period of Germany, and Marr[20] in the Ordovician of England. Antevs[21] reports varve analyses from glacial material of Permian and Precambrian age.

Varve studies confirm the occurrence of slow variations in climate. These variations may depend on small variations in solar radiation received by the earth due to cyclic changes in the orbit of the earth. These variations can also be linked to the alternation of climatic phases during the Pleistocene. The most complete scale showing this correspondence was drawn up by Milankovitch.[22] According to this scale the beginning of the Pleistocene fell 600,000 years before the present. This estimate is in remarkably good accord with calculations by Penck and Bruckner, who used rates of erosion and sedimentation.[23] Milankovitch thought his calculations might be in error by 5 percent. Allowing for various uncertainties in the effects of radiation on the earth, this is a minimum figure, probably a considerable underestimate. All estimates based on the duration of the Pleistocene contain at least this error.

Another method of time computation, conceived by Halley (1656–1742), is based on geological processes. This method assumes that the oceans were originally fresh water, and have become salt through the influx of sodium and chlorine derived from the land. The method was first attempted by Joly, who obtained an age of 80 million years for the ocean waters.[24] The objections to the method are very grave. The geochemical cycle of sodium is imperfectly known. The rates at which sodium is added to and subtracted (as salt beds) from the ocean are very poorly known. The rates at present may have nothing to do with those in the past. Taking into account all these uncertainties, Conway[25] has reexamined the method and gives 700 million years as a minimum age of the oceans and 2,350 million years as a maximum. Considering the present doubts as to the origin and nature of the primeval ocean, the method has little merit.

All of the methods thus far mentioned had been used before 1900–generally in a crude way. During the 1890s the duration of the Phanerozoic was widely accepted as several hundred million years. The duration of the Precambrian was unknown. Lord Kelvin, the most influential physicist of the day, deriving his opinion from the supposed cooling of the earth, claimed that the earth could not be more than 200 million years old, and probably was about 40 million years old.[26] Despite Kelvin's prestige, this view was very generally rejected by geologists as giving too little time for the working out of earth history.

Hardly had Kelvin's views received their final form, when they were overthrown by the discovery of radioactivity. Radioactive disintegration supplied an undreamed-of source of heat, and made it plain that the earth was not cooling at any appreciable rate and might indeed be heating up. The study of radioactive decay opened up revolutionary vistas in the study of the age of rocks. In order to understand these implications a short review of radioactivity follows.

Matter is composed of atoms, which are in turn composed of smaller particles. Electrons, very light, negatively charged particles, form a cloud surrounding a very dense, small core called the nucleus. The nucleus is composed of heavy particles called protons and neutrons, cemented together by a bewildering array of other particles which may, for our purposes, be ignored. The properties of an atom are determined by the number of electrons (which is always the same as the number of protons). Thus iron for example has 26 protons and 26 electrons, but it may have anywhere from 26 to 33 neutrons. Since in the atomic mass scale protons and neutrons have weight one, these atoms would be called iron^{52} to iron^{59} respectively. Each atom with properties of iron is called an *isotope* of iron. Thus iron has eight *isotopes.*

Latest compilations list over 1,100 isotopes of 104 elements. An isotope may be either stable, meaning that we can detect no change in its properties over a long period of time, or it may be unstable. If an isotope is unstable, its nucleus breaks down by expelling particles of various types.[27] Generally these particles are of three types; alpha particles which are composed of two protons and two neutrons, beta particles which are electrons, and gamma particles which are high energy radiation. An atom losing any one of these particles is transformed into a different type of atom, which may in turn be unstable. Eventually, however, decay will produce a stable residue. This is called a *daughter product.*[28]

Measurements of hundreds of isotopes show that radioactive disintegration proceeds in a definite way. For each isotope, there is a time "t" in which one half the atoms break down. This time is characteristic of the isotope, and is called the "half-life." The half-life is the time in which one half of the original atoms decay. Thus after time "t," one half the original atoms are left; after time "2t," one quarter are left; after "3t," one eighth are left and so on.

A consideration of the nature of radioactive decay shows

that the half-life for alpha, beta, and gamma decays must be very insensitive to alterations in temperature, pressure, or chemical combination. Chemical effects occur almost entirely in the electron shell and leave the nucleus unaffected. The nucleus is millions of times as dense as ordinary atoms; hence the effect of pressure will be extremely small. In theory, if the pressure were raised high enough, the electrons could be stripped off the nucleus, and the atoms of nonmetals would take on many of the properties of metals. In metals the nuclei are surrounded by a cloud of freely moving electrons. This pressure cannot be reached in present experimental apparatus, and calculations show it probably cannot be attained within the earth.

Similarly, raising the temperature will eventually strip off the electrons. However, temperatures required to strip common elements of electrons are of the order of 10,000°C or higher. It is extremely unlikely that such temperatures exist within the earth. Hence we conclude that radioactive decay has probably taken place at rates unaltered by extranuclear influence since the formation of the earth as an independent body. This is not to say that radioactive decay cannot be altered under any circumstances. On the contrary, present astrophysical theory holds that in the interior of stars atoms are smelted down and their constituent parts reassembled. But the earth is not a star, and the conditions within stars could not exist in a body the size and composition of the earth.

The constant rate of radioactive decay provides an ideal geological clock. By measuring the amounts of radioactive isotopes and daughter product(s), it is easy to calculate when the emitter was last separated from its daughter products. This clock has the great advantage in that its working can be examined in the laboratory. For every type of decay, there are isotopes with half-lives varying from fractions of seconds to many years. Thus each type of decay can be examined over any fraction of its lifetime, and we may convince ourselves that, for example, all beta decays are analogous. They do not vary in rate over, say 10 half-lives. This negates arguments which suppose that the rate of radioactive decay varies in some way over its lifetime. It also provides a firm foundation for measurements on very long-lived isotopes which can only be observed over a minute fraction of their half-life. Subject to the basic scientific assumption that matter does not arbitrarily change its properties, and subject to the further assumption that very slow progressive changes in the nature of matter have not been overlooked, radioactive decay forms a highly accurate clock.

From the point of view of physics there seem to be no loopholes in the use of radioactive clocks, although the concept of radioactive decay involves some conceptual difficulties. First, the idea that identical atoms break down at widely varying times violates the classical concept of causality. This violation has led to a general abandonment of the classical form of causality in favor of a statistical type of causality. Second, the erratic spacing of radioactive disintegrations shows the necessity for "coarse graining" reality. By this we mean that phenomena must be *averaged* over considerable periods of time in order for trends to become visible. This concept is fundamental to modern physics, and refutes older views of the nature of process and causality.

From the point of view of geology, however, the practical difficulties are considerable. First, for practical purposes an isotope may be used for events covering 0.01 to 10 times its half-life. This is not a theoretical limitation, but results from the difficulty of measuring extremely minute amounts of emitter and daughter products. The isotopes used at present, together with their half-lives are shown in Table 2 in Appendix I. Note that none of the half-lives fall between a few thousand and several hundred million years. The estimated age of the earth is such that a natural radioactive isotope cannot exist in detectable amounts unless it either has a half-life greater than about 50 million years, or else is continually replenished. Thus carbon^{14} would long since have disappeared, except that it is continually replenished by the reaction of cosmic rays with nitrogen^{14} in the upper atmosphere.

No useful active isotopes with half-lives in the range 100,000 to 1,000,000 years are known at present. This creates a serious gap in the radiometric time scale extending from about 500,000 years to about 10,000,000 years. Efforts are being made to fill this hiatus by improving the potassium-argon technique. However, the results of these efforts must be viewed with caution in view of the analytical difficulties.

Carbon^{14} dating is important since it provides a link between historical times and the geological past. The method is used on remains of once living organisms, on the assumption that the isotopic composition of their carbon was originally the same as the present isotopic composition of carbon. There are a number of difficulties in the carbon^{14} technique. First it assumes that the average strength of cosmic radiation was the same in the past as it is now.[29] Further, the possibility of isotopic exchange reactions is ignored. If carbon^{14} is brought in contact with a compound containing ordinary carbon^{12}, a reaction may occur in which some of the carbon^{12} exchanges place with the carbon^{14}. For instance charcoal (almost pure carbon) may react with carbon dioxide in the air:

carbon^{14} + carbon^{12} dioxide = carbon^{12} + carbon^{14} dioxide

Due to the time required for the oceans to come to equilibrium with the atmosphere, some of the carbon^{14} has decayed before it is incorporated in seawater, and thus the atmosphere has a different C^{14}/C^{12} ratio than the ocean. The rate of release of nonorganic carbon^{12} into the hydrosphere and atmosphere (chiefly from the decomposition of carbonate rocks) is uncertain. All these factors may be expected to alter the ages obtained by this method. With all these disturbing factors we might expect carbon^{12} dating to be unreliable, but Table 2 shows substantial agreement between carbon^{14} dates and historical dates of well-dated historical objects. In all except one case, the error is less than 5 percent. Of course a table such as this should not be understood to mean that *all* radiocarbon dates conform with other data. There are numerous discrepancies. Radiocarbon dating, however, has proved sufficiently reliable to become a routine tool in archaeology.

A number of difficulties, both physical and geological, occur in dating with the other isotopes mentioned. The physical difficulties concern the determination of extremely long half-lives. Glendenin estimates that the values for the half-lives of potassium^{40} and rubidium^{87} are not known with accuracy greater than 5 percent.[30] Potassium^{40} has the additional complication that it can decay through two different decay schemes, and the ratio in which these decays occur must be found (branching ratio).

Geological conditions required for age determination are the following. (1) A mineral is required to be present in detectable amounts of emitter and daughter element. (2) The mineral must originally either be free of contamination by daughter elements, or else such contamination must be measurable. (3) The mineral must be unaffected by geological events later than those which are to be dated.

The mineral used for radioactive dating depends on the technique used. Table 3 shows most of the isotopes presently in use and under research, together with their half-life, the ages for which they are applicable, and the minerals which can be measured. Muscovite and biotite are micas occurring very commonly in igneous and metamorphic rocks. Glauconite is a micalike mineral occurring in sedimentary rocks. High hopes were held for it in dating sedimentary rocks by the potassium-argon method. However, it has proved generally unsuitable for this purpose because of a disordered structure which permits escape of argon. Interest has revived with the advent of the rubidium-strontium method which avoids this problem. Uraninite, monazite, and zircon occur in trace amounts in most crystalline (as opposed to sedimentary) rocks. Sylvite is potassium chloride, occurring in salt deposits. Galena and pyrite are sulphide minerals very commonly associated with ore deposits. The other methods mentioned are in the developmental stage and are of dubious utility.

The elimination of contamination material may be handled in two ways. First, a mineral can be selected for dating which quantitatively excludes the daughter element during crystallization. An example of this is the calcium^{40} method in sylvite. In sylvite, calcium is totally excluded from the lattice when the mineral crystallizes. Hence calcium^{40} found by analysis must arise from the decay of potassium. Second, the level of contamination may be measured by using an internal standard. This standard may be of two types. In the case of lead, one isotope, lead^{204}, is not known to arise by radioactive decay. If it is supposed that all present-day lead has grown from primeval lead by the addition of radiogenic lead, an equation can be constructed giving the age of emplacement in terms of the age of the earth (To). In principle "To" can be found from one sample of lead dated by other methods, but in practice the ages determined for "To" are very dependent on the age of emplacement which is difficult to determine accurately.

Another method for eliminating error of this kind is to measure isotope ratios in a mineral containing the daughter but not the parent. Thus a mineral which contains strontium, but no rubidium, supposedly shows the original strontium isotope ratio in this rock. This method is also used for some work with the lead method. A disadvantage is the assumption that no serious isotopic fractionation takes place between different minerals. There is no reason to assume that the ratio of strontium^{87} to strontium^{86} is not different in different minerals.

The selecting of materials for age dating is an art rather than a science. Obviously altered or crushed material is avoided. Careful microscopic examination will generally disclose alteration or incipient metamorphism which can result in aberrant calculated ages. Metamorphic rocks, particularly in the region of masses of younger rocks intruding them, commonly give spuriously young ages; that is, they give the age of the latest metamorphism rather than the time of formation of the rock. By dating various minerals with different resistances to metamorphism it is sometimes possible to discern various metamorphic "overprints" on a rock.

One other method of age dating has recently been developed which uses radioactive materials in a novel form. Uranium gives off highly energetic particles when it disintegrates. These particles are shot through the surroundings and leave a trail of disorganized material behind them. In glasses this trail can be made visible by etching the glass with dilute acid. By counting these tracks and analyzing the glass for uranium it is possible to compute an age. The method is really a novel method of analyzing for the fission products of uranium with extremely high sensitivity. Quite literally single atoms of fission products are counted. This method, which is still in the development stage, appears particularly useful in the range from zero to 10 million years, where other methods are weak.

The accuracy of radioactive age dating depends on a number of factors. Glendenin [30] states that decay constants for potassium^{40} and rubidium^{87} are known with accuracy of

5–6 percent. The case for uranium isotopes is probably somewhat better. Analytical errors also enter into this evaluation, particularly when one operates at the extreme range of a method. These errors, combined with mass spectrometer errors, probably aggregate to at least 10 percent possible error and considerably more in an individual case. The analytical errors can be substantially reduced by replicate analyses, but it seems safe to estimate that there are few measured ages greater than 100 million years for which the possible error is less than 10 percent.

To compare these errors to more familiar time scales: if we say the time is a quarter to three (meaning it is between 22 minutes to three and eight minutes to three) the possible error is 15 minutes out of 12 hours, or about 2 percent. If we say we went to work yesterday at eight o'clock, meaning between 7:45 and 8:15, the possible error is half an hour or 4 percent. If we allow our watch might be 5 minutes in error, the total possible errors would be 3 percent and 5 percent respectively.

On examining any computed geologic age, two questions arise: (1) What does it mean?, and (2) How reliable is it? The significance of the first question may be seen from the parallel question "How old is this book?" One might answer it is so many days since I bought it; or alternately it is so many months since it was printed; or again that it is so many years since the manuscript was completed; or again that it is so many years since the manuscript was conceived. All of these figures are significant, and we must have clearly in mind which one we wish to know, or confusion will result. With a geologic age we must ask whether it shows the general age of the surroundings, the age of one small intrusive body, the age of some period of reheating after the original formation of the rock, or some different, possibly ill-defined event.

Now suppose that we have a number representing an age. We have decided what the possible analytical errors are in the number, and we have decided exactly what event it is supposed to date. How can we tell whether this date is reliable? Scientists make this decision by considering how consistent the date is with other data. Consistency may be either internal or external. If we took 10 samples from the same outcrop and dated each of them by various methods, and all dates were the same (within the possible error of the method), these data would be internally consistent. Another test of internal consistency is to date the same sample by several different methods. Some data of this kind are shown in Table 4. Such data are very strong evidence that the derived date is correct. It is extremely difficult to imagine any process or even a combination of processes which could alter several heterogeneous chemical systems in a congruent manner.

It may also be possible to compare a radiometric age against data external to the dated rock. In Table 1 (p. 88) is shown the Phanerozoic time scale. This scale is constructed from the "best" values of various kinds: internally consistent data which are obtained from well-defined stratigraphic points. Now if we date a rock from a lava bed between two rock layers both of which contain lower Permian fossils, we expect the date to be 250–270 million years. Allowing a possible error of 10 percent, if the date is not between 225–295 million years, it is inconsistent. As yet this kind of test can only be applied to Cambrian or younger rocks. For Precambrian rocks we can only apply the test of internal consistency.

How consistent is radiometric dating? Internal and external consistency are virtually always found together, that is, if a set of data are internally consistent they almost never conflict with the external data. Internally consistent data are not particularly common however. Because dating is done for such a variety of purposes and by a variety of methods there are no reliable compilations of figures, but a reasonable estimate would be that at least half of the data for which comparative data are available show inconsistencies of one kind or another. There is a systematic discrepancy of about 5 percent between potassium-argon and rubidium-strontium data even where other data are consistent. This discrepancy is thought to show an error in determination of the physical constants of either potassium^{40} or rubidium^{87}, but the error has not yet been identified.

Some systematic discrepancies of other kinds can be identified by graphical plotting. In Figure 1 (p. 91) is shown a "concordia diagram" for uranium-lead age determinations. If the data were all consistent they should all fall on this curve at a point equivalent to the age. However many data fall under the curve. The "x's" show schematically the data for a series of samples from one area. These data are discordant or inconsistent. Note however that they fall on a straight line. It can readily be shown that such a pattern is produced by loss of lead from a rock of age "A." These data therefore yield an age even though they are inconsistent.

A similar plot is shown in Figure 2 for rubidium-strontium. In this case the straight line is called an isochron, and its slope defines an age. With certain assumptions, one point is enough to define an isochron, but several points (from different minerals, or from different rocks) give a line which gives a reliable age even though some of the points have noticeable inconsistencies.

Many other discrepancies are due to asking questions which the data cannot answer. For example, we take potassium-argon, rubidium-strontium, and uranium-lead dates from the same rock and find them all different. If we expected them all to give the same date, we would be disappointed. If we realize that the uranium-lead date gives the original date of formation of the zircons, the rubidium-strontium date tells when the rock was recrystallized, and the potassium-argon date represents a relatively recent reheating of the rock to a few hundred degrees centigrade, then it becomes clear that the data are not inconsistent.

When we eliminate data in which the inconsistencies demonstrate the operation of well understood physical causes, and those in which the data can be plausibly, if not quantitatively explained by physical processes indicated by other data, the amount of genuinely discrepant data is small. This body of discrepant data contains the shortcomings of the theory of geological age dating, as well as various outright mistakes in measurement or interpretation.

The smallness of this body of discrepant data, the almost invariable association of internal and external consistence, and the general concordance of radiometric dates with the less exact nonradiometric dates, have led to a very general agreement that radiometric dating can, under favorable conditions, yield dependable dates for geologic events.

Note that evidence of external consistency is generally confined to fossiliferous rocks, and that nonradiometric methods of dating are also strongly dependent on fossiliferous rocks. For this reason dates from Precambrian (nonfossiliferous) rocks are inherently less dependable than those in younger rocks. The age of the lowest Cambrian rocks is thought at present to be about 600 million years. This is a relatively young age compared to those yielded by many Precambrian rocks. There are a large number of Precambrian ages clustered about each of the figures 1,000 million, 1,700 million, 2,400 million, and 3,000 million. There are a smaller number of ages rising as high as 3,800 million years. External evidence of the great age of these rocks is difficult to obtain.

Three general methods of finding the age of the earth (and thus the duration of Precambrian time) have been proposed. Two of these date the formation of the earth as an independent body, or perhaps some event in its very early life, while the third gives an idea of the age of the solar system. The first argument notes that a considerable part of the lead content of the earth arises by decay of uranium isotopes. Some equations showing the relations between the present abundance of lead isotopes, the age of the earth, and the lead isotope ratios at the time of origin of the earth are shown in Appendix I. As already noted, the age of the earth can be found in principle from a single sample of lead of known geologic age. This is called the "terrestrial lead" method. Generally large numbers of terrestrial leads are used to find the age of the earth. A variation of the method is to measure the lead isotopes in nonradioactive meteorites ("cosmic lead" method) which are believed to be debris left from the formation of the planets. Both of these methods give results very close to 4.55 billion years. This is believed to be the most accurate current estimate of the age of the earth.

A second method of finding the age of the earth is to date meteorites directly. The resultant dates tend to fall in the range 4–4.5 billion years with a scattering of younger dates down to a few hundred million years.

The third method of estimating the age of the earth depends on astrophysical theory. According to current theories stars obtain their light from thermonuclear reactions which convert hydrogen to helium. By measuring the hydrogen to helium ratio in a star, which can be done by measuring the light which it emits with a spectrograph, the age of a star can be estimated. Some current estimates place the age of the sun between 5–10 billion years. The difficulty with this method is that the light from a star comes from its outer portions. It is not obvious that the outer portions of the star have a composition representative of the whole body, even assuming efficient convection.

The final limit on time scales also comes from astrophysical theory. There is now general agreement that the universe is expanding. Various attempts to evade this conclusion have failed, and the evidence now seems conclusive. By extending this concept into the past, it may be calculated that 7–10 billion years ago all the matter in the known universe was in a very small volume. Now there is no known way to stop the collapse of such a tremendous mass of matter. Gravitational collapse will cause the density to rise to extreme values. Under such conditions the concept "time" simply breaks down. No meaning can be attached to the concepts "simultaneous" or "consecutive." This is known in cosmological terms as a "singularity." It can be called in simple terms the creation of the universe.

At present astrophysical theory is in reasonable concord with the hypothesized age of the earth. This has not always been the case. It was only a few years ago that the age of the universe was widely thought to be only 3 billion years. This was the result of erroneous determinations of the distance to various stars. Astrophysical theory has undergone numerous other radical changes in the past two decades. In these circumstances the concord between astrophysical theory and geologic age dating, while encouraging belief in the dates obtained, is not strong evidence of the correctness of either theory.

Recently another astrophysical method has been found which supports to some extent the geological time scale. Certain types of corals show conspicuous ridging on their shells. The larger ridges are annual growth rings. The smaller appear to be daily rings. Wells, using this assumption and carefully counting, believes that the number of days in a year, 365 at present, amounted to 415 in the Devonian period (400 million years ago). Now it is well known that the length of the day is gradually increasing due to transfer of momentum from the earth to the moon. This transfer results from friction between the oceans and the land during tidal motions, which are of course largely caused by the moon. If the present rate of lengthening is projected backward, it is found that there should be in fact about 415 days per year during the Devonian period. This assumes that one year is the length of time required for the earth to pass around the sun and return to the same place in the orbit, and that this period of time remains constant. Wells has shown that from the present back to the Devonian the agreement between astronomic theory and coral ridges is excellent. The method cannot be pushed further back because of the lack of suitable fossil material. This particular method is of theoretical significance because it connects the geological time scale to (a) the stratigraphic time scale (established from fossil evidence) and (b) astronomic theory.

In conclusion, the Phanerozoic time scale (the time since the appearance of abundant fossils) rests on (a) radiometric age dating, (b) stratigraphic dating, a relative scale but one of great accuracy, (c) geological "clocks" (sediment accumulation and the rest), and (d) astrophysical theory. Agreement between these four is sufficiently good to justify the conclusion that it is extremely unlikely that the time scale will change by more than 10 percent. Proposed alterations to this scale must take into account not only radiometric dates but the other factors as well. No known or proposed process could alter these congruently. The Precambrian time scale, on the other hand, rests almost entirely on radiometric dating, with weak support from astronomic theory. Considerable changes seem quite possible here, perhaps of the order of 25 percent or even more. The current estimate of the age of the earth according to these scales is 4.55 billion years.

NOTES

1. F. Zeuner, *Dating the Past, An Introduction to Geochronology*, 4th ed. (London: Methuen and Co., 1958), p. 3.
2. Robert Hooke, *Discourse on Earthquakes* (London, 1668).
3. C. Lyell, *Principles of Geology*, 1st ed., II (London, 1830).
4. C. Lyell, *Principles of Geology*, 10th ed., I (1867), 300–301.
5. W. D. Matthew, "Time Ratios in the Evolution of Mammalian Phyla," *Science* (New York), XL (1914), 232–35.
6. J. D. Dana, *Manual of Geology*, 2nd ed. (New York, 1876), 828 pp.
7. C. D. Walcott, "Geologic Time as Indicated by the Sedimentary Rocks of North America," *J. Geology*, I (1893), 639–76.
8. M. Reade, *Chemical Denudation in Relation to Geologic Time* (London, 1879), 61 pp.
9. J. G. Goodchild, "Some Geological Evidence Regarding the Age of the Earth," *Proc. Roy. Phys. Soc. Edinburgh*, XXXI, sec. 3 (1897), 259–308.
10. J. Barrell, "Rhythms and Measurement of Geologic Time," *Bull. Geol. Soc. America*, XXVIII (1917), 745–904.
11. C. Schuchert, "Geochronology, or the Age of the Earth on the Basis of Sediments and Life," *Bull. Nat. Research Council*, Washington, No. 80 (1931), pp. 10–64.
12. A. Holmes, "The Construction of a Geological Time Scale," *Trans. Geol. Soc. Glasgow*, XXI (1947), 117–53.
13. R. A. Sonder, *Mechanik der Erde* (Stuttgart, 1956), 291 pp.
14. A. E. Douglass, "The Secret of the Southwest Solved by Talkative Tree Rings," *National Geographic Magazine*, LVI (1929), 737–70.
15. R. Liden, "Geochronological Studies on the Finiglacial Stage in Angerman Land," *Sverige geologisks Untersolkse*, Stockholm, IX (1913), 1–39 (in Swedish).
16. G. de Geer, "A Geochronology of the Last 12,000 Years," *Comptes Rendu, XI Congress geologique, Internationale*, Stockholm (1910), pp. 241–253.
17. M. Sauramo, "The Mode of Land Upheaval in Fennoscandia During Late Quaternary Time," *Compte Rendues, Soc. geol., Finlande*, XIII (1939), 1–26.
18. E. Antevs, "Late Glacial Clay Chronology of North America," *Rept. Smithsonian Inst. of Washington* (1931), pp. 313–24.
19. H. Korn, "Schichtung und absolute Zeit," *Neues Jahrbuch Mineralogie, Stuttgart*, Band 74A (1938), 50–186.
20. J. E. Marr, "A Possible Chronometric Scale for the Graptolite Strata," *Paleobiologica*, Wien, I (1928), 161–62.
21. E. Antevs, "Retreat of the Last Ice-Sheet in Eastern Canada," *Memoir 146, Geol. Survey Canada* (1925), p. 142.
22. M. Milankovitch, *Astronomische Mittel zur Erforschung der Erdegeschichtlichen Klimate, Handbuch der Geophysik*, IX (1938), pp. 593–698. A recent review of the theory is given by W. Broeker in *Science*, CLI (1966), 299–304.
23. A. Penck and E. Bruckner, *Die Alpen in Eiszeitalter* (Leipzig, 1909), 1189 pp.
24. J. Joly, *The Geological Age of the Earth as Indicated by the Sodium Content of the Sea* (8 p. pamphlet), (Dublin, 1900).

25. E. J. Conway, "The Chemical Evolution of the Sea," *Proc. Royal Irish Academy*, XLVIII (1943), pp. 161–212.
26. Sir W. Thomson (Lord Kelvin), "The Age of the Earth as an Abode Fitted for Life," *Philosophical Magazine*, XLVII (1899), pp. 66–90.
27. Some relatively rare types of radioactivity also involve the extra nuclear electrons, for example, orbital electron capture.
28. All of the products resulting from radioactive decay are termed daughter products, whether stable or not.
29. Several attempts have been made to prove this assumption. Compare W. Dyck, "Secular Variation in C^{14} Abundance of Douglass Fir Tree Rings," *Canadian J. Earth Sciences*, III (1966), pp. 6–7.
30. L. E. Glendenin, *NATO Symposium on Radioactive Dating* (Athens, 1961).

Appendix

Table 1

Geological Time Scale According to Two Compilers

Era	Period	Epoch	Kulp	Holmes
Cenozoic	Quaternary	Pleistocene	1 (million)	1
		Pliocene	12	11
		Miocene	23	25
	Tertiary	Oligocene	35	40
		Eocene	55	60
		Paleocene	70	70
	Cretaceous	Upper	90	
Mesozoic		Middle	120	
		Lower	135	135
	Jurassic	Upper	150	
		Middle	170	
		Lower	180	180
	Triassic	Upper	200	
		Middle		
		Lower	220	225
	Permian	Upper	235	
Paleozoic		Middle	250	
		Lower	270	270
	Pennsylvanian	Upper		
		Middle		
		Lower	320	
	Mississippian	Upper		
		Middle		
		Lower	350	350
	Devonian	Upper	365	
		Middle	380	
		Lower	400	400
	Silurian		430	440
	Ordovician		490	500
	Cambrian		600	600

See H. L. Kulp, "The Geological Time Scale," *Int. Geol. Cong. Rept.* 21 session, pt. 3 (1960), pp. 18–27. A. Holmes, "A Revised Geological Time Scale," *Trans. Edinburgh Geol. Soc.* XVII (1959), pt. 3, pp. 183–216.

Table 2

Comparison of Historic Ages and Carbon-14 Ages

Object	Historic age	Probable error in historic age	C^{14} age
Mammal remains (Peru)	444	25	450
Sequoia tree ring	880	15	930
Douglas fir ring	1372	50	1100
Sequoia tree ring	1377	4	1430
Roman ship	1990	3	2030
Wood from case of Egyptian mummy	2280		2190
Etruscan charcoal	2600	100	2730
Redwood tree ring	2928	53	3005
Wood from Egyptian tomb	3750		3621
Egyptian tomb	4575	75	4817
Egyptian tomb	4900	200	4883

(After *McGraw-Hill Encyclopedia of Science and Technology,* XI [New York: McGraw-Hill Book Co., 1960], 295.)

Table 3

Methods of Radioactive Age Dating

Decay	Half life (years)	Useful time-span	Minerals used	Usefulness
$Rb^{87}–Sr^{87}$	6.0×10^{10}	10^8–To	M, B, Gl, (Ks) lepidolite	very useful
$K^{40}–A^{40}$	1.4×10^9	10^7–To	M, B, Gl, (Ks) whole rock	very useful
$U^{235}–Pb^{207}$	7.1×10^8		uraninite, zircon	useful
$U^{237}–Pb^{205}$	4.5×10^9	~10^8–To	monazite uraniferous	for special purposes
$Th^{232}–Pb^{208}$	1.39×10^{10}		shale	
C^{14}	5570	0–50,000	carbonaceous biogenic material	very useful for prehistoric era
$K^{40}–Ca^{40}$	1.4×10^9	10^7–10^9	sylvite	very limited
Pb–Pb		10^8–10^{10}	galena, pyrite	doubtful accuracy for age work
Cl^{36}	4×10^5	?	chlorine rich material (salt)	none as yet
H^3	12.5	0–50	groundwater	good for special purpose
Radiation damage (fission tracks)		0–10^8(?)	zircon, glass	doubtful

Decay	Half life (years)	Useful time-span	Minerals used	Usefulness
Ionium	1670	0–10,000	deep sea ooze	doubtful
Re^{187}–Os^{187}	4×10^{12}	$>$109 (10^9)	molybdenite	very dubious
Lu^{176}–Hf^{176}	7.5×10^{10}	$>5\times10^8$	rare earth minerals	very dubious
Ra^{231}–Th^{230}	34,300	0–250,000	deep sea ooze	probably useful

M – muscovite; B – biotite; Gl – glauconite; Ks – potash feldspar
To – age of the earth (about 4.6 billion years)
$>$ greater than, $<$ less than
$\backsim$ – equivalent to

Table 4

Selected examples of Rocks Dated by Different Minerals and Different Methods

	K/A	Rb/Sr	U/Pb^{208}	U/Pb^{207}
Redstone, N. H.	2500M	2740M	2600U	2640U
Keystone, S. Dak.	1570M	1490M	1610U	1620U
Wilberforce, Ont.	960B	1020B	1020U	1020U
Wichita Mts., Okla.	460B	510B	517Z	525Z
Redstone, N. H.	168B	190B	187Z	184Z

See also Lowdon, p. 120, for measurements of the same kind
B – biotite; M – muscovite; U – uraninite; Z – zircon

Table 5

Comparison of the Age of Minerals from the Same Rock Sample GSC 59-87 Pegmatite dyke, Lac Pied des Monts, Quebec

Mineral	Pb207/206	207/U235	206/238	208/232	K/A
Uraninite	1020	980	975	-	
Muscovite					935
Biotite					925

In this specimen, which is one of a series of about 50, it has been possible to measure five independent ages from three different minerals. All agree within experimental error (5%). It is extremely difficult to imagine a process which could fortuitously give rise to congruent results of this kind. (Example taken from Lowdon, *Geological Survey of Canada,* Paper 61-17 [1961], p. 119.)

"Concordia" curve for lead isotopes. Radiometric age dates determined from uranium isotopes 235 and 238 can be concordant only if the lead to uranium ratios fall on the solid line. However, many experimental data are found similar to those marked by 'x' on the diagram. The data fall on a straight line which cuts the concordia at two points. The data plotted in the figure would be interpreted as uranium emplaced 2,500 million years ago, and reheated 700 million years ago. Alternately it could be interpreted as 2,500 million-year-old material which steadily lost lead, possibly by diffusion. The concordia also shows graphically why lead-uranium methods are accurate for old ages, but inaccurate for ages less than a few hundred million years. The upper left corner is too crowded for high accuracy.

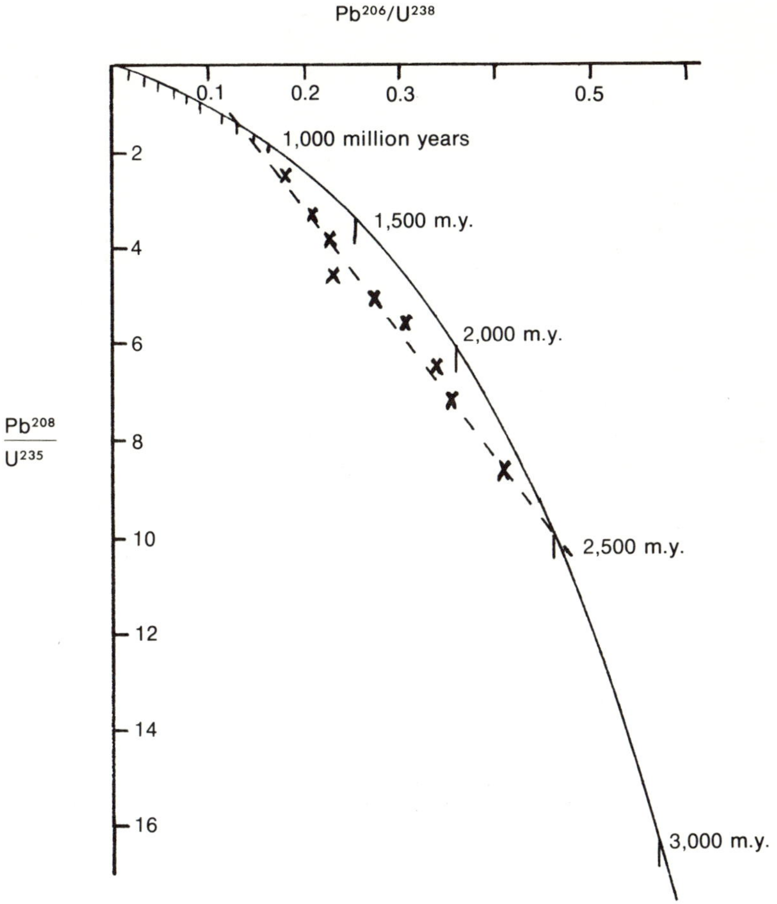

Fig. 1

Isochron plot of rubidium-strontium data for Precambrian rocks from the Front Range of Colorado. The full circles, to which the solid line is the best fit, define an age of 1,750 million years, with (Sr^{87}/Sr^{86}) of 0.7079. Note that even though individual points fall slightly off the line, the slope of the line is well defined. The possible error in determination of slope corresponds to an error of about 30 million years in age. The data plotted on the dashed line are from younger (by field evidence) metamorphic rocks with an isochron age of 1,350 million years, and $(Sr^{87}/Sr^{86})_0$ of 0.725. Note that the age is defined by the *slope* of the line passing through the points (compare Figure 1), and that the initial strontium isotope ratio is found from the data, not assumed.

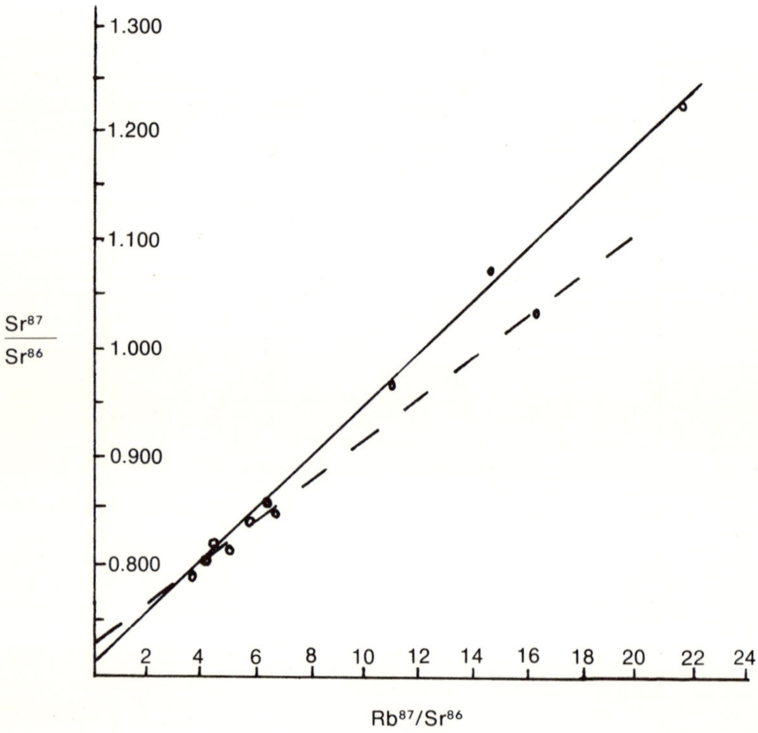

Fig. 2

Section III

The Affirmations of Holy Scripture Concerning Creation

6 • The Biblical Account of the Creation

Fred Kramer

In the versions read by most Christians the Bible opens with the simple yet magnificent statement: "In the beginning God created the heaven and the earth." Then it pictures in quick succession the ordering of the universe by the creation of light, the establishment of day and night, the fixing of the firmament, and the separation of the waters from the land.

After this it recounts in order the creation of plants, the heavenly bodies, and the animal world, with the order proceeding from marine animals through birds and land animals, both tame and wild, and ending with the creation of man.

The concept of time enters this brief description of the creation with the mention of day and night.

Not all editions of the Bible render Gen. 1:1 as it is translated in the Authorized and the Revised Standard versions of the English Bible. The Smith-Goodspeed version translates: "When God began to create the heavens and the earth, the earth was a desolate waste." [1]

The Smith-Goodspeed translation does not stand alone in translating the first verse of the Bible in this way. The Anchor Bible translates similarly and says in a note: "It is worth noting that the majority of Hebrew commentators and grammarians, not to mention many moderns, could see no objection to viewing Gen. 1:1 as a dependent clause." [2]

The difficulty in agreeing on the best manner of translating Gen. 1:1 arises from the fact that the ancient Hebrew language was written without vowels. People who were familiar with the language could read it without great difficulty. Some centuries after the beginning of the Christian era Jewish scholars added the vowels for greater ease in reading the text. In a few Scripture passages there is some question about the proper vowels, and Gen. 1:1 is one of these passages. Scholars are divided as to the proper vowels in this case. Hence the difference in translation.

A number of highly respected Old Testament scholars speak for the translation as we have it in the Authorized and in the Revised Standard versions of the English Bible. The famous commentators Franz Delitzsch [3] and Von Rad [4] favor the translation of the Authorized Version. The same is true of the Jewish scholar Umberto Cassuto.[5]

The rendering, "When God began to create," etc., has been used by some conservative scholars in an attempt to find a place in Genesis 1 for the long ages posited by uniformitarian geologists. The Scofield Reference Bible may serve as a case in point. While it retains the translation of the Authorized Version, it places a new heading after Gen. 1:1, "Earth made waste and empty by judgment" (Jer. 4:23-26). To verse 2, "And the earth was without form and void," it adds the footnote:

> Jer. 4:23-26, Isa. 24:1 and 45:18, clearly indicate that the earth had undergone a cataclysmic change as the result of a divine judgment. The face of the earth bears everywhere the marks of such a catastrophe. There are not wanting intimations which connect it with a previous testing and fall of angels. See Ezk. 28:12-15 and Isa. 14:9-14, which certainly go beyond the kings of Tyre and Babylon.

Scofield assumes that Gen. 1:1 records the original creation, and that after Gen. 1:1 must be placed a very long period of time during which took place the testing and fall of the angels, which was accompanied by a catastrophe in which the first creation was wrecked. This view assumes that the fossils of prehistoric monsters belong to that earlier creation destroyed at the fall of the angels. What is reported after Gen. 1:2 is then viewed as a recreation or restoration.

Scofield's note on verse 1 says:

> But three *creative* acts of God are recorded in this chapter: (1) the heavens and the earth, v. 1; (2) animal

life, v. 21; and (3) human life, vs. 26, 27. The first creative act refers to the dateless past and gives scope for all the geologic ages.

The view here expressed by the Scofield Bible finds favor with some conservative Bible students. It must, however, be pointed out that the text does not speak of a "time gap" between Gen. 1:1 and the rest of the chapter. Furthermore, there is nothing in Scripture to indicate that the fall of the angels took place at this juncture. Neither do the passages adduced from Isaiah and Jeremiah "indicate . . . a cataclysmic change as a result of a divine judgment" at the time of Genesis 1 but rather the punishment of the Lord upon Israel, for whose sin the land is reduced to a state such as it was in when the earth was "without form and void" and not yet inhabited by man and beast.

Eduard Koenig appears to be on firm ground when, after discussing the pros and cons with respect to the two possible translations of Gen. 1:1, he says:

> The restitution hypothesis [that is, the hypothesis that Gen. 1:3-27 tells of the re-creation of a world destroyed by the fall of the angels] has no basis whatsoever in the text.[6]

The reader who approaches Genesis 1 without prejudice is not likely to find in this brief chapter anything more or less than an account of the original creation of the universe, its ordering by the creation of light, the firmament, the sea and the heavenly bodies, its adornment by the plant world, followed by the creation of the animal world, including man. If there is a great time interval or gap in the history of the primeval world, it is passed over in Genesis 1.

The time during which the creative acts of God took place is given as six days, with the length of the days unspecified. However, the weight of the evidence (each morning followed by an evening) favors normal days.

The whole account of the creation covers scarcely more than one page in most editions of the Bible. This is followed in Genesis 2 by an even briefer account stating in somewhat more detailed fashion the creation of the first man and woman and the preparation of their first home in the Garden of Eden.

The physical and biological sciences of our day posit the origin of the earth some 4½ billions of years ago by means of indeterminate forces, and the development by natural processes extending over hundreds of millions of years of those things which in Genesis 1 are described as having been created by God in six days.

Ever since the rise of the natural sciences in the 17th and particularly in the 18th and 19th centuries, some theologians and also some scientists have sought to harmonize Genesis 1 and 2 with scientific theories concerning the origin of the universe and of all forms of life.

Prominent among proposals for harmonization have been attempts to make the six days of Genesis 1 long periods of time, so that each day represents a geological period. Others have advanced the aforementioned "gap theory," which places a long time between Gen. 1:1, 2 and the remainder of the chapter, into which gap the geological ages are supposed to fit.

These and similar attempts all seek to impose something on the text which is not there. A Christian who attempts to solve his difficulties with scientific theories in this fashion should not be accused of heresy. These are in a very real sense exegetical questions. But neither dare anyone demand that an explanation which happens to satisfy him be accepted by others who find the explanation unacceptable for exegetical or scientific reasons.

In the running battle which has been and continues to be fought between theologians and scientists over questions connected with the creation there have been and are many scientists who are humble Christians, and there have been and are theologians who are knowledgeable in the field of science. There have also been theologians who have spoken dogmatically where their knowledge neither of Scripture nor of science qualified them to do so; and there have been men of science who have spoken dogmatically, only to be proven wrong in their own field by later developments. It is a fact that man's knowledge, including the knowledge of scientists and theologians, even in their own fields of competence, is at all times fragmentary. Also the understanding which theologians have of the Scripture is but "in part." (1 Cor. 13:9)

Largely through the work of the advocates of the higher historical and literary criticism, theologians have come increasingly to realize the genuine difficulty of understanding fully the true meaning particularly of ancient texts, coming as they do out of strange, long-dead cultures.

Literary critics have pointed out the importance of recognizing the literary genre of any ancient writing—if the writing is to be correctly understood. Every intelligent reader knows that it is important for the understanding of a piece of literature to know whether it is sober history or a poem or a parable or a fable, etc.

The question of the literary genre of the Biblical account of the creation is of utmost importance for its correct understanding and use. The question of the literary genre of the early chapters of Genesis has received much attention in recent times from Biblical scholars, but the scholars have by no means been of one mind on the question.

It seems certain that the ancient Jewish authorities understood the story as sober history. The same is true of the church fathers during the early centuries of the Christian church. So also Luther understood these chapters when he wrote his great commentary on the Book of Genesis. So it was generally understood by generations of Lutheran theologians after Luther's time.

From this understanding of the story some concluded that deductions with respect to scientific questions could be *freely* drawn from statements in the Biblical account of creation. Attempts were made by theologians to fix the age of the universe, the nature of the universe, the position of the earth in the universe, the precise length it had taken God to create all things, and the fixity of species.

Scientists who studied the universe, the earth, and the forms of life on earth empirically and, where that was possible, experimentally, often reached conclusions different from those which theologians believed they could draw from Genesis 1, and conflict inevitably followed between scientists and theologians.

With the development of the higher literary and historical criticism during the 18th and 19th centuries the question of literary genre, which had not greatly troubled exegetes before this time, suddenly assumed great importance. It became fashionable to assume that much in Scripture, particularly in the Old Testament, is myth. Myth was generally not carefully defined, and there are also today a number of different definitions of myth. To begin with, the term myth was generally understood in a negative sense, as something that is not true, and therefore of little if any value.

Today myth is considered by some Biblical scholars as an important literary genre, and at times great value is placed on myth. It is understood as in no sense history, but as a story which may teach a very important truth. It is considered a teaching device, and it can be demonstrated that it was so used by the ancients.[7]

The high estimate some ancient and some modern scholars place upon myth as a teaching device is not shared by Holy Scripture. The Pastoral Epistles contain warnings against giving attention to myths. 1 Tim. 1:3-4: "Charge certain persons not to teach any different doctrine, nor to occupy themselves with myths." Titus 1:13-14: "Therefore rebuke them sharply, that they may be sound in the faith instead of giving heed to Jewish myths." 1 Tim. 4:7: "Have nothing to do with godless and silly myths." 2 Tim. 4:3-4: "The time is coming when people will not endure sound teaching, but . . . will turn away from listening to the truth and wander into myths." St. Peter assures his readers that the apostles were not preaching myths but facts. 2 Peter 1:16: "We did not follow cleverly devised myths when we made known to you the power and coming of our Lord Jesus Christ, but we were eyewitnesses of His majesty."[8]

When higher critics first began to consider much in Scripture to be mythical, they tended to look on the early chapters of Genesis as Babylonian myths which the Jews had learned during the Babylonian captivity and introduced into the Pentateuch. They supposed much of the latter to have been written during or even after the Babylonian Captivity. However, it has been conclusively shown that this is not the case.

Alexander Heidel, a scholar at the Oriental Institute of Chicago University, examined the stories from Babylon which appeared to parallel the story of the Creation and of the Flood in the Book of Genesis and came to the conclusion that much in the Babylonian stories is indeed myth. The stories are highly polytheistic and tell many things about gods and goddesses that strike a person at once as being mythical. But he showed that the Biblical stories are the opposite of the myths of Babylon, even though events are described in the Babylonian stories which have strange parallels in the Book of Genesis. He concluded that there are historical facts behind the so-called Babylonian myths and that the Biblical account gives us fact without myth.[9]

Biblical scholars by and large, particularly the more conservative ones, are considerably more careful today in speaking about the literary genre employed in the early chapters of Genesis. Many of them consider these chapters to be saga, that is, stories that were told orally for perhaps many centuries before they were reduced to writing. Consequently these stories are not considered to be history in the sense in which historians seek to write history today, but they are thought to have a genuine historical kernel. The following explanation by Gerhard von Rad, a contemporary Old Testament scholar, may indicate how saga is understood in contemporary Biblical scholarship:

> At first, knowledge of the long process to which individual traditions were subjected before they received their final and present form in our book of Genesis makes the work of the exegete difficult. Above all, there are two groups of hermeneutic questions that we must wrestle to answer. For a long time Old Testament science has called these traditions "sagas." Thus one of the first tasks of the exegete is to give an exact account of this term, the possibility and the limits of its use. A second task arises from the fact that the narratives, which formerly began in isolation, are now related to a large overlapping context and obviously must be interpreted within this context, from the particular spot that has been assigned to them within the

> The stark simplicity of this introductory section is thus by no means a mark of meager writing ability. It is the result of special cultivation, a process in which detail was defined through endless probing and each word subjected to minutest scrutiny. By the same token, the end product cannot have been the work of an individual, but must be attributed to a school with a continuous tradition behind it. The ultimate objective was to set forth, in a manner that must not presume in any way to edit the achievement of the Creator—by the slightest injection of sentiment or personality—not a theory but a credo, a credo untinged by the least hint of speculation.[12]

The above quotations are introduced here, *not* by way of endorsement, but to show how higher critics have changed their views concerning the nature and literary genre of the early chapters of Genesis. From the bald assumption that these chapters present myths some higher critics have come to speak of them in terms of respect. It must not, however, be assumed that the sentiments of Von Rad and of the Anchor Bible represent the last word that will come from higher critics on the nature and literary genre of Genesis 1. Just as scientists may be expected to continue to come up with new theories about the origin of the universe and of all forms of life, so theologians of critical bent may be expected to come up with new literary genres. Meanwhile, however, Christians must live their life here on earth in faith in their Creator and in obedience to Him. While scientists study the physical universe empirically and, to the extent that this is possible, experimentally, the Biblical scholars debate literary genres, Christians must seek to maintain a sane and Christian view and understanding of the early chapters of Genesis, even as they seek such a view and understanding of all Scripture.

It is important in this connection to consider the commonplace conclusion of higher critics that Gen. 1:1-2, verse 4a, and Gen. 2, verse 4b and following, constitute two independent and somewhat conflicting accounts of creation. On the basis of this conclusion many scholars assert that one cannot draw any specific information from these chapters. The best that can be done is to note that the sovereignty of God is asserted, that there is a polemic against nature gods, and that man's central position in nature is defined. But, they assert, one may not use these chapters as evidence of man's special creation versus an evolutionary development.

However, a careful examination of the first two chapters of Genesis will demonstrate that their unity can not be so easily dismissed. On the contrary, a good case may be made for the thesis that Genesis 1 and 2 are in fact a unified account in two parts. The first part gives a broad cosmological view of the entire creative act. The second part focuses anthropologically on man in his relation to God and creation.

According to the Documentary Hypothesis the use of different names for God in the two sections is strong evidence that these were originally two separate sections which at a later date were modified and joined by one or more editors. It is pointed out that Genesis 1 uses the term "Elohim" (God) exclusively, while the name "Yahweh" (Jehovah—KJV, Lord—RSV) is used in the second section beginning with Gen. 2:4b.

Umberto Cassuto, the late Jewish scholar, and others have questioned the validity of this keystone of the Documentary Hypothesis.[13] Cassuto points out that the difference in use of divine names lies not in separate sources but in the difference in the purpose of the two sections. In the first section the author paints a broad picture of creation in its totality. His emphasis is on the transcendent God of the universe. Hence the author uses "Elohim," the generic term for God. Elohim signifies the source of all power and energy, the supreme Creator. In Gen. 2:4b and following, the author uses the name "Yahweh" (Jehovah, Lord), a proper noun meaning specifically the covenant God of Israel. Yahweh recalls the moral and spiritual parts of God's character. The reason for this lies in the focus of chapter 2 on man rather than on the totality of creation.

Cassuto demonstrates that the use of divine names in Genesis follows three well defined rules: First, Yahweh is used when Scripture speaks of God in his ethical aspect and specifically as the covenant God of the Israelites. Elohim refers to God in a general sense as the almighty Creator of the material world, the God of nature, the preserver of all living things. Second, Yahweh is used when the Bible speaks of the "intuitive" notion of God as held by the people. Elohim is used in more philosophically oriented discussions. Third, Yahweh appears when God is presented in his personal relationship to men and nature. Elohim tends to point to God as the Transcendent One who stands outside and above nature.[14]

On the basis of these rules of Scriptural usage of the divine names, it may be concluded that Elohim is used naturally in the first section of the creation story, whereas the second section logically calls for the introduction of the name Yahweh. Thus we conclude that the use of different names provides no reason for denying the unity of the section.

Space does not permit a full treatment of the question of the unity of the creation account. However, attention must be given to the assertion of higher critics that Genesis 1 and 2 contain contradictions and hence must come from different accounts. Two examples will show that the alleged contradictions do not have a basis in fact.

Exponents of the Documentary Hypothesis say that the first section teaches creation in six days, but that the second section instead teaches creation in only one day (Gen. 2:4, "In the *day* that the Lord God made the earth and the heavens.") In answer it may be said that the phrase "in the day" does not specifically signify a day of twenty-four hours either in Hebrew or English. For example, in Num. 3:1 we read "in the *day* that the Lord spoke with Moses on Mount Sinai," (KJV). Actually Moses remained on Mount Sinai 40 days and 40 nights. Hence "in the day" merely means "at the time" or "at the period." Thus there is no contradiction in time between Genesis chapters 1 and 2.

A second alleged inconsistency is that Gen. 1:27 informs us that two sexes were created simultaneously ("male and female created He them"), but the second section relates that Adam was formed first (Gen. 2:7) and Eve afterwards (Gen. 2:21-22). But this example also does not prove to be a contradiction when one studies the Biblical way of relating events. The Semitic method often involved making a complete general statement first and then going back and providing a more detailed elaboration. For example, in Gen. 28:5 we are told: "Thus Isaac sent Jacob away, and he went to Padan-Aram to Laban, the son of Bethuel the Aramean." In the verses that follow (6-9) we are told of Esau's reaction. The story then goes back prior to this reaction, returns to Jacob's journey and describes it in detail: "Jacob left Beersheba and went toward Haran, and he came to a certain place, etc." (v. 10-11). The same principle applies in the creation story. After telling the whole story in summary fashion (Gen. 1), the author returns to the account of man's creation and in detail tells how Adam was created first and then Eve. Again, no real discrepancy is involved. The unity of the two sections remains.

What may—what must a Bible-believing Christian hold concerning the early chapters of Genesis? He must hold that also these chapters, like all Scripture, are given by inspiration of God (2 Tim. 3:16), and that they are therefore God's infallible Word.

It must be evident to every thinking Christian that Genesis 1 and much of Genesis 2 cannot be eyewitness accounts as are many accounts in the historical books of the Old Testament and in the Gospels and the Book of Acts. There was no man present in the beginning, when God created the heaven and the earth, and filled it with creatures. Genesis 1 is either, as higher critics assume, the product of human minds, whether you call it myth, saga, or priestly wisdom; or it is the fruit of divine revelation. Christians throughout the ages have believed it to be the latter. They should continue to accept it as such. Any other view falls short of what Scripture has to say concerning its own nature and inspiration.

Accepting Genesis 1 as the result of divine revelation does not, however, guarantee a correct understanding or an accurate interpretation of the Biblical account of creation. In making known His Word and will to men, "God . . . at sundry times and in divers manners spake in time past unto the fathers by the prophets" (Heb. 1:1 KJV). In the various ways in which God spoke in times past He also employed various literary genres. Scripture itself tells us that in connection with the sedition of Miriam and Aaron, God called Miriam and Aaron and said: "Hear now My words: If there be a prophet among you,

I the Lord will make Myself known unto him in a vision, and will speak unto him in a dream. My servant Moses is not so, who is faithful in all Mine house. With him I will speak mouth to mouth, even apparently, and not in dark speeches; and the similitude of the Lord shall he behold." (Num. 12:6-8)

The question then arises, How is God speaking in Genesis 1? The following points are worthy of careful consideration:

First, the language of Genesis 1 is not obscure or purely poetic and figurative, but descriptive, simple, and clear.

Second, the language is not, however, scientific language as this is understood today. It has been called "phenomenal" language because it describes things, not as science has learned to describe them, seeking to explain the specific cause and effect relationship behind a happening, but as events appear to the observer who is without explicit scientific knowledge and instruments.

Thus in verse 7, "God made the firmament, and divided the waters which were under the firmament from the waters which were above the firmament." In verses 14-18 we are told that God said:

> Let there be lights in the firmament of the heaven to divide the day from the night; and let them be for signs, and for seasons, and for days, and years: And let them be for lights in the firmament of the heaven to give light upon the earth; and it was so. And God made two great lights; the greater light to rule the day, and the lesser light to rule the night; He made the stars also. And God set them in the firmament of the heaven to give light upon the earth, And to rule over the day and over the night, and to divide the light from the darkness. (KJV)

The heavens are here described as they appear to one who views them from the earth, not as they appear to one who studies them with all the means at the disposal of modern science.

Finally, it must also be said that the language is sometimes anthropomorphic, that is, it speaks of God in human terms, as though He had a human form and other human attributes. In verses 26-27 we read:

> And God said, Let Us make man in our image, after our likeness; And let them have dominion over the fish of the sea, and over the fowl of the air, and over the cattle, and over all the earth, and over every creeping thing that creepeth upon the earth. So God created man in His own image, in the image of God created He him; male and female created He them.

The language becomes more anthropomorphic in Genesis 2 where God forms man of the dust of the ground, and breathes into his nostrils the breath of life. This anthropomorphic language is very prominent in the Old Testament.

The use of anthropomorphisms in the Old Testament in no way calls into question the historicity or the correctness of the Biblical accounts. On this subject we quote from an essay by Paul Zimmerman, entitled, *The Word of God Today:*[15]

> An examination of the use of anthropomorphisms in the Bible leads to the conclusion that their presence in an account does not "ipso facto" render the account a figurative or poetic account. For example, in Genesis 11:29 we read, "It came to pass when God destroyed the cities of the plain that God *remembered* Abraham." The fact that the anthropomorphic expression "remembered" is used does not take away from this historical account that the cities were actually destroyed. In Exodus 3:8 God says, "I am come down to deliver them out of the hand of the Egyptians." Again the fact that God is spoken of as coming down does not mean that there was no deliverance out of the bondage of Egypt. Similarly Christ, in Luke 11:20 says, "By the finger of God I cast out demons." The reference to the finger of God would certainly not mean that the casting out of the demons is something which did not actually take place. We would conclude that it takes something more than the presence of an anthropomorphism to render an account nonprose and nonfactual.

Any person who is inclined to take offense at the language of Genesis 1 and to impugn the correctness of the account ought to give thought to the following facts. When

God gave His Word to man, He aimed to be understood. He adapted the form of the message to the understanding of the people to whom it was addressed. It appears very certain that, had God chosen to speak to His people in days of old in what we now consider scientifically accurate language, men could not have understood Him.

If we assume for instance that God had given the accounts in Genesis in the language of the science of the present day, even scientists of centuries past would have been greatly puzzled. If on the other hand such an account written in terms of the science of the present day were to be read by scientists a few centuries hence, they would without doubt smile and feel that the account was very far behind the times.

The Word of God was given in order that it might teach God's children of every age. The first men who read Genesis 1 learned from it the supremely important fact that God is their Creator, and they His creatures, made in His image and therefore responsible to Him, are in duty bound to live as men made in the image of God.

This has been the message of Genesis 1 throughout the ages. It is the same for the scientific scholar and for the layman in scientific matters. Both can get the message. Both will be able to get the message hundreds of years hence.

Because of its very nature, scientific reasoning cannot properly criticize the Biblical account of creation. Creation speaks of the time when God was in the process of establishing the universe and natural law. Moreover, by its very nature, science is always in flux. As scientists discover new data in their empirical study of the universe scientific theories will be modified. Some may be discarded entirely. In spite of great advances in scientific discovery and scientific thinking, scientists stand before a riddle when they ask, not about the observable phenomena of the universe, but about its first cause. The answer to this riddle is found in Gen. 1:1, "In the beginning God created the heaven and the earth."

Theologians on their part should recognize the true nature and purpose of Genesis 1, and not use this chapter to try to establish scientific theories of their own by an appeal to the Word of God. Genesis 1 is the opening chapter of that Book which according to its own testimony, was given "by inspiration of God," to "make men wise unto salvation through faith which is in Christ Jesus." When this book speaks on topics in which science is also interested, it must be believed. Its primary purpose is not, however, to instruct men with respect to scientific questions but to teach men the saving knowledge of God in Christ.

On account of its very nature and purpose the Bible leaves many scientific questions regarding the Creation unanswered. But what it teaches concerning the Creation is of the utmost importance for the Christian faith. Therefore also the New Testament harks back again and again to the early chapters of Genesis as it sets forth the Christian faith for the salvation of men.

The Creation is referred to by Christ when He speaks of the terrors which will accompany the destruction of Jerusalem: "In those days there will be such tribulation as has not been from the beginning of the creation which God created until now . . ." Mark 13:19 (RSV). St. Paul, speaking of the fact that the Gospel is to be preached to the Gentiles, says that for ages this mystery was hidden "in God who created all things," Eph. 3:9. The same apostle teaches that the Creator can be perceived in a measure by what He has created. "Ever since the creation of the world His invisible nature, namely His eternal power and deity, has been clearly perceived in the things that have been made." (Rom. 1:20)

The New Testament speaks of Adam and Eve as real, historical persons. In the genealogy of Christ, Luke 3:23-38, Christ's ancestry is traced back to Adam, who is called the son of God, vs. 38. St. Paul is evidently drawing on Gen. 2:7, 18, 21-23 when he writes: "Adam was formed first, then Eve." (1 Tim. 2:13)

The New Testament teaches that the human race originated from the creation by God of one man and one woman. With evident reference to Genesis 1, Christ says: "From the beginning of creation God made them male and female. For this reason man shall leave his father and mother and be joined to his wife, and the two shall become one," Mark 10:6-7. With an evident reference to Genesis 2, Paul writes: "Man was not made from woman, but woman from man. Neither was man created for woman, but woman for man." (1 Cor. 11:8-9)

Scripture moreover teaches that this first human pair was not primitive, nor apelike, but created in the image of God. This teaching of Gen. 1:27 is alluded to and therefore recognized and approved in the New Testament teaching concerning the new man in the Christian. "Put off your old nature which belongs to your former manner of life and is corrupt through deceitful lusts, and be renewed in the spirit of your minds, and put on the new nature, created after the likeness of God in true righteousness and holiness," Eph. 4:22-24. "You . . . have put on the new nature, which is being renewed in knowledge after the image of its Creator." (Col. 3:9-10)

The New Testament also contains unmistakable references to the fall of the first human pair as related in Genesis 3. Speaking of Adam and Eve, St. Paul writes, "Adam was formed first, then Eve; and Adam was not deceived, but the woman was deceived and became a transgressor," 1 Tim. 2:13-14. The same apostle writes to the Corinthians, "I am afraid that as the serpent deceived Eve by his cunning, your thoughts will be led astray from a sincere and pure devotion to Christ." (2 Cor. 11:3)

The serpent which deceived Eve is identified by the New Testament with the devil. In the Book of Revelation, which pictures among other things the fight of the archangel Michael with the devil, the holy writer says, "And the great dragon was thrown down, that ancient serpent, who is called the Devil and Satan, the deceiver of the whole world . . ." Rev. 12:9. "And he seized the dragon, that ancient serpent, who is the Devil and Satan, and bound him for a thousand years." (Rev. 20:2)

The deceiver of the first human pair is consistently pictured as the tempter in the New Testament. He tempts the Son of God Himself, Matt. 4:1 ff.; he tempts the followers of Christ, who must be on the lookout for him. (Eph. 6:11; 1 Peter 5:8)

The result of the fall of Adam, according to the New Testament, is universal death. "As sin came into the world through one man and death through sin . . . so death spread to all men because all men sinned." (Rom. 5:12)

The New Testament, which pictures the Creation as lying

under the curse of death because of the sin of Adam, also knows of a yearning of the Creation for redemption. "The Creation waits with eager longing for the revealing of the sons of God; for the Creation was subjected to futility, not of its own will but by the will of Him who subjected it in hope; because the Creation itself will be set free from its bondage to decay and obtain the glorious liberty of the children of God. We know that the whole creation has been groaning in travail together until now . . ." (Rom. 8:19-22)

The redemption of mankind from its fallen state, in which it is subject to sin and death, is the purpose of the coming of Christ the eternal Son of God, into man's flesh. "The reason the Son of God appeared was to destroy the works of the devil," 1 John 3:8. Christ, whom the New Testament calls the second Adam in contrast to the first, who brought death into the world by sin, is called by St. Paul "a life-giving spirit." (1 Cor. 15:45)

Those who by faith in Christ's redemption are in Christ have been rescued from their wretched state in which, as sons of Adam, they lay, subject to sin and death. They are now called, in the New Testament, new creatures. "Therefore, if any one is in Christ, he is a new creation; the old has passed away, behold, the new has come," 2 Cor. 5:17. The restoration of the divine image, lost by the fall of Adam, is begun in them. Therefore they are admonished, "Put off your old nature which belongs to your former manner of life and is corrupt through deceitful lusts, and be renewed in the spirit of your minds, and put on the new nature, created after the likeness of God in true righteousness and holiness," Eph. 4:22-24. "[You] . . . have put on the new nature, which is being renewed in knowledge after the image of its Creator." (Col. 3:10)

Those who have become new creatures by faith in Christ are taught by the New Testament to look forward to the day when the heaven and earth that now is will pass away, 2 Peter 3:10, and God will create "new heavens and a new earth in which righteousness dwells." (2 Peter 3:13)

So we find that the early chapters of Genesis, with their account of the creation of heaven and earth, of Adam and Eve, and of the fall into sin, are firmly woven into the texture of the Christian faith and of the New Testament.

Notes

1. *The Complete Bible: An American Translation,* the Old Testament trans. James M. Powis Smith et al., the New Testament by Edgar J. Goodspeed (Chicago: University of Chicago Press, 1939).
2. *The Anchor Bible, Genesis* (Garden City, N. Y.: Doubleday and Co., 1964), p. 12.
3. C. F. Keil and R. Delitzsch, *The Pentateuch, Vol. I* (Grand Rapids, Mich.: Wm. B. Eerdmans Pub. Co., n.d.). "Bereschith (in the beginning) is used absolutely. . . . The following clause cannot be treated as subordinate . . . by rendering it, 'in the beginning when God created . . .' etc." They maintain that this would be "opposed to the grammar of the language." (P. 46)
4. Gerhard von Rad, *Genesis,* trans. John H. Marks (Philadelphia: The Westminster Press, © 1961, by W. L. Jenkins, used by permission), p. 46. Von Rad says in his comment on the passage: "We do not follow the old conjecture that v. 1 is not to be understood as an independent sentence but as the introductory clause to v. 2 or even to v. 3 ("at the beginning when God created heaven and earth . . ."). Syntactically perhaps both translations are possible, but not theologically."
5. Umberto Cassuto, *A Commentary on the Book of Genesis* (Jerusalem: The Magnus Press, The Hebrew University, 1961). Cassuto quotes Jewish authorities for the translation, "at the beginning, . . . when the earth was without form and void," but argues against this in favor of the absolute rendering, "In the beginning God created the heaven and the earth." (P. 19)
6. Eduard Koenig, *Genesis* (Guetersloh: C. Bertelsman, 1919), p. 134. "Diese Restitutionshypothese hat indes im Texte gar keinen Anhalt."
7. An example of the use of myth as a teaching device is found in Plato's "Protagoras," *The Dialogues of Plato,* trans. Benjamin Jowett, Great Books of the Western World, VII (Chicago: William Benton, Encyclopaedia Britannica, Inc., 1952), pp. 44–45.
8. All Scripture passages quoted according to the Revised Standard Version.
9. Alexander Heidel, *The Babylonian Genesis* (Chicago: University of Chicago Press, 1942).
10. Von Rad, *Genesis,* pp. 30–31.
11. Von Rad, pp. 61–62. Used by permission.
12. *Anchor Bible, Genesis,* Introduction, trans. and ed. E. A. Speiser (Garden City, N. Y.: © Doubleday and Co. Inc., 1964), p. 8.
13. Umberto Cassuto, *A Commentary on the Book of Genesis* (Jerusalem: Magnes Press, Hebrew University, 1961–64), p. 85.
14. Ibid., p. 87.
15. Paul A. Zimmerman, "The Word of God Today," in *Essays From the Creationist Viewpoint,* ed. Paul A. Zimmerman (Ann Arbor, Mich., 435 Pine Brae, 1966), p. 35.

SECTION IV

The Geological Record

7 • Overview of the Geological Record

Kenneth L. Currie

Compared to human historical documents, rocks are very old. If the rocks could tell us their history, we would see very far back into the past. However, most rocks were formed under conditions very unlike those presently prevailing on the surface of the earth. Attempts to reconstruct their history are uncertain at best, and mere speculation in most cases. However, some rocks are being formed at present on the surface of the earth. Small particles are gradually being accreted on the floor of the oceans (pelagic ooze), on beaches (sand), in deserts (sand, loess), under glaciers (till, moraine), surrounding volcanoes (ash, lapilli). These deposits of sediment are slowly indurated by loss of water and chemical reactions to form rocks. Because they are deposited in successive layers on an underlying surface, these sedimentary rocks tend to form successive, nearly horizontal layers. However, some sedimentary rocks may have the form of long, narrow belts (consider a beach turned into a rock). Others may have a wedge-like form. An example would be the material deposited by landslides at the base of a cliff.

Among the rocks exposed for study by geologists are many which resemble solidified deposits of recent sediments. Using the principle of uniformity, geologists assume that the sediment in these rocks accumulated by processes which we can observe today. Information can be extracted from the rocks about the processes and conditions in operation during the formation of the rock. This amount of "history" can be derived from the rocks. Information is chiefly gained from four characteristics of the rock; (a) fossil content, (b) composition of the particles, (c) texture of the rock, and (d) structure of the rock.

The fossil content of a rock has two highly important uses: (1) correlation of rocks from different areas and (2) information on the conditions under which the rock was formed. The uses of correlation can be understood from a simple example. Suppose oil is found in rock layer A and in no other. Now we wish to drill a hole to layer A and no further. How do we tell when the drill has reached layer A? The answer is found in the fossil content of layer A. This has been found by 150 years of experience to be a highly reliable guide to identification of rock layers. Not only can it be used to trace a single rock layer over a limited area, but in a broad way it can be used to correlate sequences of rocks on different continents. The precision with which correlations can be made depends on the variety of fossils present. Of course it is possible that one rock layer does not have any co-relative in a distant area. This situation would arise if the corresponding layer has never been deposited or has been eroded away since it was deposited.

Fossils can be used for a quite different purpose: the determining of conditions under which the organism lived. If fossil corals are found in a certain outcrop, for example, we may deduce from the present-day distribution of corals that warm clear seas existed at that point at the time the corals were living. A large amount of information about temperature, salinity, atmosphere, and other factors can be gained from a study of the ecology of fossils.

This information can be cross-checked by comparison with data obtained from the physical character of the rocks. For example, if we find a rock containing hematite ("rust") as an essential constituent, we deduce that a certain amount of oxygen was present during formation of the rock. If on the other hand we find iron present as iron sulphide (fools gold), we deduce that very little oxygen was present. Clearly the amount of oxygen present will have a very strong effect on the kind of life that can live in an environment, and hence on the kind of fossils which will be found. Fossil content and chemical character can therefore corroborate or contradict each other. Similarly other chemical reactions are critically dependent on temperature or acidity or pressure or other variables. These factors can often be determined quite closely.

While the chemical composition can give clues to static factors involved in the formation of a rock, the *texture* yields clues to the dynamic factors. If we find many boulders, then powerful transport agents have clearly operated, perhaps landslides or powerful mountain torrents. On the other hand, rocks such as massive salt beds contain no fragmental material at all and have been deposited in a very calm environment with little or no currents. Other textural features may be: ripple marks, seen on any beach, also found in sand on the bottom of creeks; desiccation cracks, seen on drying mud banks, rain prints; graded bedding, coarse sand at the base grading to fine sand at the top of a layer; and many, many others. All of these textures have a significant meaning. They help the geologist build up a picture of conditions at the time the rock was formed.

The *structure* of a rock is the shape imposed on it after the original accumulation of sediment. An idea of the significance can be gained by taking 10 to 20 sheets of paper and twisting them into various shapes, allowing a few rips here and there. Layered sedimentary rocks can be forced into all of these shapes. Complex structure makes it difficult to determine the original sequence of beds; it distorts fossil and textural evidence and may cause chemical changes in the rock. The forces causing complex structures are not completely understood. Some structures can be caused by gravity sliding. Soft beds may be thrown into very complex folded structures in this way. A model of this process can be made by sliding a thin sheet of putty down an oiled glass plate and allowing it to pile up at the bottom. Other structures are due to vertical movements of rocks beneath them. This type of structure can be modeled by moving wooden blocks up and down under thin sheets of putty or clay. At one time it was thought that most structures were due to lateral compression or tension of the rocks. This view has been abandoned for all large structures. The mechanism will not work for the same reason you cannot push a sheet of wet Kleenex—it will crumple around the pusher, and the force can only be transmitted a short distance.

Assuming that we are able to unravel the structural complexities (which can be a formidable task), each observed sequence of sedimentary rocks yields information about a restricted span of time. By piecing together all the available information we can build up a picture of how the surface of the earth changed throughout time. This composite picture is termed the "geological record." We can tell for example how continents rose and fell, how temperatures changed, and how plant and animal life changed. Of course this record is at best fragmentary and incomplete. At no known place in the world has deposition of sediments taken place continuously. There are always gaps in the record. Sedimentary rocks comprise less than 0.1 percent of the volume of the earth. The geological record of which we are speaking tells us nothing directly of the other 99.9 percent. These objections are inherent in the nature of the available data. As we have seen, these data are not entirely independent of each other. In many cases it is possible to use one kind of data to check another. A significant test of the usefulness of historical geology is whether it yields a self-consistent picture.

No large body of scientific data is totally self-consistent. Internal contradictions may be ascribed to two causes. On the one hand are errors of observation or interpretation. On the other hand are shortcomings of theory. The former are a kind of "noise," a nuisance which cannot be totally gotten rid of nor totally disregarded. It is always possible that what we call today a mistaken measurement may tomorrow turn out to be the correct one. Science advances on its mistakes. The data which stubbornly refuse to be either explained or disregarded are the basis of new theories. These new theories may either be old ones slightly modified to fit the new data, or they may be totally new concepts.

In the case of the geologic record we have seen that, apart from basic assumptions outside the body of science, the record depends on (1) an ordering of the sedimentary units in order of age, which is based almost entirely on fossil evidence, and (2) identification of conditions of deposition from present physical conditions. The internal contradictions which can arise are therefore twofold, either a breakdown in the ordering of sedimentary units or an apparently impossible condition of origin.

As we have seen, identification of the position of a bed is based on comparison of its fossil content with worldwide catalogs of fossils. Let us suppose that the world sequence of beds *can* be labeled A, B, C, D . . . in order of decreasing age. Now if in a particular area we found the sequence A, C, D, this is not an anomaly. Bed B was either not deposited or has been eroded away. However, the sequence A, C, B, D is definitely anomalous and requires explanation. Of course a sequence, D, C, B, A, is even more anomalous. Anomalous sequences do not necessarily imply a breakdown in the ordering of the sedimentary units. There are many ways in which such anomalies can arise. For example, take a sheet of paper and mark an X on one edge. Hold the edge with the X steady and push the other edge toward it. The paper will crumple and eventually the X will be on the bottom of one of the crumples. This is known technically as an overturned fold and produces the sequence D, C, B, A.

Another method of producing a similar result can be visualized by opening a book and piling up some loose sheets of paper beside the sloping edge. Now suppose the loose sheets are identical in age to the sheet of the book at a corresponding level. If we shove on the edge of the loose sheets, they will slide up over "younger" sheets in the book. This is technically called an "overthrust" and can produce sequences of type A, B, C, AB, C. Sheeted rocks are particularly subject to overthrusting because the layers slide easily over each other. Although our simple analogies have used pushing to make the structures, it seems more likely that in nature the rocks move under the influence of gravity, not lateral compression.

In addition to structural dislocations of the stratigraphic column, anomalies in the succession can arise in other ways. Fossils are in many cases hard resistant objects. In some cases they may weather out of their enclosing rocks and be incorporated in younger sediments. A well-known example is occurring in New Jersey where fossil shellfish are weathering out of sea cliffs and being incorporated in contemporary sands. This process appears to interpolate a much older bed into a series of young rocks.

The reverse process is also possible. Small organisms can penetrate remarkable distances into rocks along cracks. Where earth movements are active, pieces of younger rocks may be physically forced into older rocks. In either case a much younger rock appears to be in the midst of old rocks.

By the processes just outlined we have seen that it is possible to reverse all or part of a sequence, to repeat the same sequence several times, to find apparently younger rocks in the midst of older ones, and to find apparently old rocks in the midst of young ones. No other types of anomaly are known in the stratigraphic succession. However, to say that anomalies *can* be caused by these processes is a very different proposition from saying that they *are* caused by this process. The operation of the various processes has been demonstrated in a few examples. They are *assumed* in a great many other similar cases. This is dangerously sloppy thinking. An anomaly in the stratigraphic succession should be clearly identified and explained.

The second type of anomaly, an apparent contradiction among the data indicating the origin of the rocks, is generally found in a limited area, but can be quite spectacular. Some examples are: the presence of extreme numbers of abraded mammal bones in some lake beds of Mesozoic age, the cross-cutting lenses of sedimentary rocks. the apparent interfingering of highly oxidized and highly reduced rocks. In the cases where these apparent contradictions have been satisfactorily resolved new concepts have been introduced.

A case in point is the turbidity current concept. In essence this idea supposes that a thin mud flows down low slopes on the ocean bottom, usually set in motion by an earthquake. This type of phenomenon has been reproduced in the laboratory, and it has been shown that the grain size of the products decreases from bottom to top of the deposit. This type of feature was previously thought to appear only in shallow water deposits, and many deep-sea deposits therefore appeared to present both deep and shallow water characters.

The recognition of turbidity current deposits has resolved a number of anomalies on the geological record.

Although many anomalies have been resolved by the introduction of new ideas and evidence, the number of unexplained anomalies has tended to grow with the growth in geological knowledge. Do the anomalies and exceptions invalidate the conclusions drawn from the geologic record?

In the first place anomalies and exceptions are relatively rare. Those which cannot be satisfactorily explained or are not dubious because of poor data are very rare indeed. The concept of the geologic record is therefore highly *useful*; that is, it incorporates a large amount of knowledge into easily assimilated form. This usefulness is the reason for the widespread acceptance of the framework of historical geology. If we could devise another theory which explained more of the geologic data than the present framework of the geologic record, and was in accord with other sciences, the geologic record would be replaced.

Now the geologic record as presently understood is based on three fundamental concepts: (1) The stratigraphic time scale is highly reliable. (2) The sedimentary sequence is built up by the slow accretion of consecutive layers. (3) The material building sedimentary rocks is deposited in large part from slowly moving fluids. All three concepts have been attacked, but the second and third have been the object of most attention. At various times and in various forms it has been proposed that all or most of the sedimentary column was deposited in a short time under catastrophic conditions, in particular from dense, rapidly moving fluids.

After relatively brief intervals, these ideas have been rejected by the majority of geologists. However, N. L. Bowen once remarked that any geological idea which appears completely dead should be periodically examined for signs of returning life. In this spirit the concept of "flood geology" deserves a serious reappraisal. While the tenets of its more extreme supporters cannot be maintained, the idea of a universal inundation may contain the explanation of some geological phenomena.

The concept was originally rejected on the assumptions that (1) sedimentary rocks accumulate slowly, (2) the complete geological record can be assembled by combining data from enough areas; hence there is no room for either hiatuses or vast accelerations in sedimentation, and (3) the present ratio of land to ocean has always been about the same; hence a universal flood is a physical impossibility.

Combined with these scientific assumptions was a judgment that the Bible was not historically accurate; hence its account of a universal flood could not be given much weight as evidence. All of these objections to the concept of a universal flood have been breaking down in recent years. It is now recognized that sedimentation can and does take place at extremely rapid rates under suitable conditions, as shown by cities which were seaports during the Middle Ages and are now several miles inland. On the other hand there appear to be intervals when no deposition at all has been preserved. The best known is the so-called Ep-Archean interval occurring below Cambrian rocks. Others have been suggested on a worldwide or continental scale. Modern geophysical research appears to indicate that continents and ocean basins are not such permanent features as was previously thought and that conversion of continents into ocean basins is not a ridiculous concept.

On the other hand it has become recognized by theologians and historians alike that the writers of the Bible were exceptionally careful and accurate observers, although their point of view was generally different from that of a scientist or historian. The Biblical account of the flood must therefore be carefully examined to determine its historical content.

8 • "Firsts" in the Geological Record

PAUL C. TYCHSEN

The stream of life as recorded in the fossil rock record has apparently been continuous since it originated. Furthermore, the record indicates periods of abrupt environmental change in climatic or sea-water conditions. In some cases such changes brought about widespread extermination of existing life. In other situations rather sudden repopulation or the appearance of new groups dominated the scene as the changed environment apparently resulted in conditions more appealing to the newer groups of plants or animals. Continental deposits (land deposits) at times were covered with layers of marine deposits (sea deposits), and in other parts of the globe typical marine-type environments were inundated beneath terrestrial deposition. Today's landscape may appear permanent to some. One must remember, however, that the only permanent thing in nature is change. Given sufficient time, most things can and do change.

Disappearance and replacement of plants and animals often kept pace with these environmental alterations. Geographic features such as valleys, bays, islands, and portions of the continental segment each claimed their peculiar inhabitants through a portion of geologic time only to be followed by changed conditions and possibly a new group of inhabitants. It is commonly asserted that each species of plant or animal came into being just once and at a single locality. Accordingly, any organism, extinct or living, that is found in more than one locality is thought to have migrated to that region from its place of origin.

And so we find that specific groups of plants and animals

tend to succeed one another in the geological record in a fairly definite and determinable order. Each period of geologic time can be recognized and identified by its own particular group of fossils. Fossil collections from various parts of the world have substantiated this concept. The Cambrian period, for example, was characterized by an abundance of trilobites – marine organisms possessing segmented shells and averaging somewhat less than an inch in length. The Devonian period has been called the Age of Fish. (See the Appendix for time chart.) The Permian period was dominated by reptiles. Rutiodon, a phytosaur of Triassic time, appears in the fossil record only during this period, and so his fossilized remains aid in dating the rocks containing them. This animal had a length of 10 to 12 feet and resembled a modern-day alligator. Many other examples of key or index fossils could be mentioned to suggest their usefulness in this manner to the geologist. Some fossils are characterized by a very short stratigraphic range and hence make good index fossils particularly if they have a wide geographic distribution.

The reader will note that not only are periods or times of extinction mentioned on the time chart, but also that times of the first appearance of particular groups of plants and animals are observed. The Ordovician period, for example, witnessed the first appearance of fish. Land-dwelling plants and animals made an initial appearance in the fossil record during the Silurian. The first record of amphibian remains is associated with the Devonian, and the first or earliest reptile remains thus far have been found in strata of the Pennsylvanian period. Many such "firsts" punctuate the geologic time scale. Their present position on the scale represents the combined efforts of many paleontologists searching the rock record since the 18th century.

At first glance it may appear that the position of the so-called firsts on the time scale are quite rigid and that repeated discovery of new fossils will only serve to corroborate existing information. In some instances this may well be the case. However, it is quite obvious that only a small percentage (possibly 1 percent) of the rock record has been investigated thus far. Hence the position of other "firsts" may shift. We would anticipate the fact that as new evidence is uncovered—and this may require considerable time—the positions of some "firsts" on the time scale may descend further and further downward; that is, into older and older rock units. And this is the only direction in which they can possibly move, assuming that our fossil finds to date have been accurately identified.

If one carefully examines the known fossil population of the Cambrian period, he will discover that representatives of all the invertebrate phyla (animals without backbones) are represented at this early date. Hundreds of species of trilobites existed at the time as well as many representatives of the Brachiopoda phylum (marine bivalved animals). In contrast to the Cambrian, the Precambrian presents a marked paucity of fossil remains. Considering the abundance of fossils in the Cambrian and their rather sudden appearance at this time, it would seem that some of the invertebrate phyla now claiming the Cambrian as the time of their first appearance will be dislodged further down into the Precambrian. Recent discovery, for example, of a jellyfish-like animal from the Nankoweap formation of the Grand Canyon region now extends the range of the Coelenterata phylum (Hydra, jellyfish, corals) well down into Precambrian time. Questionable brachiopod shells have been similarly reported from Precambrian age strata.

Early in this century Chamberlin and Salisbury stated that:

> No traces of vertebrates have yet been detected in the Cambrian beds, but as fish remains have been found in the rocks of the following period (Ordovician) it would be hazardous to assume that the lower aquatic vertebrates were not among the denizens of the Cambrian waters.[1]

Chamberlin and Salisbury's text lists amphibians as originating during the Mississippian period, while current opinion favors placing the first amphibians in the Devonian. A Danish exploration in 1932 in eastern Greenland uncovered an upper Devonian-period deposit containing fish and the oldest known amphibians. The same reference also lists the Permian as witnessing the advent of the reptiles, while contemporary opinion places them in the earlier Pennsylvanian period.

The Chamberlin and Salisbury text also comments that there was little more than a bare indication that the echinoderms (starfish, sea urchins, etc.) were present in Cambrian time. Continued search since has confirmed the definite existence of the echinoderms during this period. It is further mentioned that Protozoa (amoebae) were probably present during the Ordovician period and could be recognized only with some uncertainty. Present-day information confirms the positive existence of Protozoa during this time. Terrestrial algae and fungi (Thallophyta) are reported still missing from the scene as late as the Devonian. Time charts nowadays extend the thallophytes back into the Precambrian. Turtles, formerly listed as appearing in the Cretaceous period for the first time, are now known to have made their first appearance in the late Triassic.

Additional evidence and continued searching of the rock record during a period of 61 years (representing the time between the publication date of the Chamberlin and Salisbury text and the present), has thus transferred some of the "firsts" into lower stratigraphic positions on the time scale. Thus these organisms lived at an earlier date than was once believed.

Pertinent literature records changes in the stratigraphic position of certain fossils, and the reader's attention is directed to a few of the more recent notations:

1. Neocalamites (Equisetales)—Remains of this plant were previously known from the Devonian to the end of the Paleozoic. This reference reports them as being found in upper Triassic age strata, although most of the remains are very fragmentary. It will be noted that in this case the stratigraphic range is extended upward.[2]

2. Ogygopsis—a trilobite genus—heretofore known in the Midcambrian and now extended downward to the upper part of the Lower Cambrian of the Canadian Rockies region.[3]

3. Eryops—a labyrinthodont amphibian. The stratigraphic range of this animal has been extended from the Permian down into the Pennsylvanian period.[4]

4. Anisus pattersoni (a freshwater snail). Earlier restricted to the Pleistocene; now found in the upper Pliocene epoch as well.[5]

5. Sphenodontids (reptiles of Triassic period) – Footprints of this reptile have now been found in Triassic period sediments, and the author contends it is only a matter of time until true fossil remains are uncovered.[6]

6. Early Seed Plants – gymnosperms – which are plants characterized by naked seeds and include the seed ferns, conifers, and cycads. Reference is made here to the fact that the gymnosperms first appear in the early lower Carboniferous periods some 250 million years ago. However, the reference states that it will not be surprising if the gymnosperms eventually are traced back to the underlying Devonian period. The author states that the first generally accepted flowering plants have been found in the mid-lower Cretaceous, but fossils that have been attributed to this group come from the Jurassic and Triassic, and a few botanists have expressed the opinion that they originated as far back as the Permian.[7]

It is apparent from the above data that the changes involving the stratigraphic position of fossils are of minor magnitude, for the most part. In other words, the first appearance of a particular fossil may be shifted downward on the time chart from one epoch to the next older epoch or from the upper horizons of one geologic system to the midportions of the same system. It is questionable whether shifts involving several periods by virtue of a single new discovery will be encountered. However, as new discoveries continue to be made, this slow displacement may result in a time span of considerable magnitude.

In recent years a new branch of plant science has developed called palynology. This is the study of the pollen grains and microspores of plants. Palynology as an organized science is possible because the ornamentation and sculpture of the surface of the pollen grains is a feature of great value for classification purposes. The outer walls of the spores being rather durable, they seldom undergo replacement or chemical alteration. They are also resistant to most forms of chemical and biological decay.

Among other features, these grains may have thin areas in their outer walls in the form of germinal pores or furrows or both. Pollen grains may then be classified as one of two possible types. The monocolpate, with one germinal furrow, occurs in monocotyledons, cycads, cycadeoids, and seed ferns, as well as some woody dicotyledons. The tricolpate type with three germinal furrows is found in most dicotyledons.

After these features of pollen grains were recognized, attention was given to the Pleistocene peat and lacustrine (lake-bed) sediments in an attempt to reconstruct the flora of the time on the basis of pollen grains present. This procedure was extended to the Tertiary formations of western Nebraska to similarly determine the grasses present at the time of their deposition.

Palynologists have been able to assign microspores that have been found in Cenozoic and Mesozoic rocks to modern families, modern genera, and sometimes to modern species of the plant world. The statistical comparison of "pollen rains" of the present to fossil pollen distribution and counts has been the basis of attempts to estimate the abundance of fossil parent plants at the time of deposition of sediments.

As the techniques of palynology were refined, it became possible to extend the study of fossil microspores into Paleozoic formations. Leclerq[8] has reported a marked discrepancy between the flora of the Middle and the Lower Devonian, and this discrepancy has been very difficult to reconcile with theories of plant evolution previously proposed. The discrepancy would seem to preclude the evolution of the Lower Devonian flora into that of the Middle Devonian in the short time interval available.

However, even more startling was the discovery of microspores of lycopods in the Middle Cambrian rocks of eastern Siberia. Since then some 50 types of microspores of vascular (woody) plants have been found in the Cambrian (the Paleozoic rocks in which all invertebrate groups suddenly appear). This evidence was first thought to be the result of contamination. However, it has since been supported by the finding of fragments of woody cells. These show the characteristic simple and bordered pits of tracheids which are characteristic of present-day conifers.

We would thus seem to be encountering further evidence for persistence of type once referred to by O. Kuhn.[9] Furthermore, the evidence for a varied land flora in the Cambrian would certainly suggest the possibility of a varied terrestial fauna in that period also.

At this point the reader's attention is directed again to the geologic timetable in the Appendix and particularly to the current position of the various "firsts." As mentioned earlier, with continued searching of the stratigraphic record it seems certain that more of the "firsts" will descend down the scale and in some cases shorten the time span between their positions. Of course it is also possible that while one "first" may be found in time to occupy a position lower on the time scale, it will be separated by virtue of its shift from another "first" higher up on the stratigraphic scale by a correspondingly greater amount of time. We anticipate that the times of the first appearance of the various animal and plant groups will be in close juxtaposition in time.

Note that the first terrestrial or land plant fossils appeared during the Silurian period, while the fossilized evidence of the first birds is now assigned to the Jurassic. This time span represents some 260 million years on the time chart. With the exception of pollen grains discussed above, plants, particularly in the early states, are ill fitted for preservation as fossils. Protective bark, husks, and shells would be absent in primitive plants, and furthermore the harsh terrestrial or land environment would not be conducive to preservation. Weathering and erosion would tend to destroy all evidence of plant life.

Similarly, the remains of both pterosaurs (flying reptiles) and birds are rare since both possessed light and very delicate skeletons. Both no doubt lived and died in forest lands which would not be favorable for the preservation of animal life as fossils. Considering then the nature of the fossil record of these two groups, it is impossible to follow the stream of land life with the same continuity as has been attempted for marine life. The record is considerably more imperfect. The oldest fossil finds must then suffice to establish only a temporary position for these particular firsts.

Much work remains to be done before the record is complete. Teichert estimates that 10 million species of plants and animals may be preserved in the rock records.[10] He further contends that the known record may represent not more than 1 percent of the potential. Future fossil finds may, in some instances, further confirm existing information as to the positioning of "firsts" and in other instances may show need to change the position. In the situations where the position is changed, the change may well be one in which the amount of time between successive firsts is appreciably shortened. The object of science is the acquisition and subsequent organization of factual knowledge. We have attempted here to examine the scientific evidence as it is currently portrayed. If the information so obtained would appear to disagree with the Biblical account, the question then is not one of inerrancy of Scripture but rather of interpretation both of Scripture and of the geological record. On the other hand, if the amount of time between the successive "firsts" is significantly reduced, this may well suggest the situation to be expected on the basis of the Genesis account of creation interpreted as a true account of the origin of life on this planet.

Notes

1. Thomas C. Chamberlin and Rollin D. Salisbury, *Geology, Vol. 2: Earth History* (New York: Henry Holt and Co., 1907), p. 280.
2. *Journal of Geology,* LV, No. 6 (Nov. 1947).
3. *Journal of Paleontology,* XXXVII, No. 9 (Jan. 1963), p. 244.
4. *Journal of Paleontology,* XXXII, No. 5 (Sept. 1958), p. 918.
5. *Journal of Paleontology,* XXXII, No. 6 (Nov. 1958), pp. 1149–59.
6. *Journal of Paleontology,* XXXVIII, No. 1 (Jan. 1964).
7. *Science,* CXLII, No. 3594 (Nov. 15, 1963).
8. S. Leclerq, "Evidence of Vascular Plants in the Cambrian," *Evolution,* X, No. 2, pp. 109–13.
9. O. Kuhn, "Typologische Betrachtungsweise und Paläontologie," *Acta Biotheoretica,* VI (1942), 55–96.
10. Teichert, "How Many Fossil Species?" *Journal of Paleontology,* XXX (1956), 967–69.

Appendix

Time Chart Commonly Used in Geology

Era	Period	Epoch	Features	Years Ago
Cenozoic	Quaternary	Recent	Modern man	11 thousand
		Pleistocene	Early man; northern glaciation	.5 to 3 mil.
		Pliocene	Large carnivores	13 ±1 mil.
		Miocene	First abundant grazing mammals	25 ±1 mil.
	Tertiary	Oligocene	Large running mammals	36 ±2 mil.
		Eocene	Many modern types of mammals	58 ±2 mil.
		Paleocene	First placental mammals	63 ±2 mil.
Mesozoic	Cretaceous		First flowering plants; climax of dinosaurs and ammonites, followed by extinction	135 ± 5 mil.
	Jurassic		First birds; first mammals; dinosaurs and ammonites abundant	180 ± 5 mil.
	Triassic		First dinosaurs; abundant cycads and conifers	230 ± 10 mil.
Paleozoic	Permian		Extinction of many types of marine life; glaciation	280 ± 10 mil.
	Pennsylvanian		First reptiles; great coal beds, conifers	310 ± mil.
	Mississippian		Sharks and amphibians abundant; numerous scale trees and ferns	345 ± 10 mil.
	Devonian		First amphibians and ammonites; abundant fish	405 ± 10 mil.
	Silurian		First terrestrial plants and animals	425 ± 10 mil.
	Ordovician		First fish; invertebrates dom.	500 ± 10 mil.
	Cambrian		First abundant record of marine life; all phyla (invert.) present	600 ± 50 mil.
Proterozoic	Keweenawan			
	Huronian			
Archeozoic	Algoman			
	Timiskaming			
	Laurentian			

After N. D. Newell, *Scientific American,* Feb. 1963, CCVIII, No. 2, p. 80.

9 • Human Fossils

Wilbert H. Rusch Sr.

I. Introduction

In almost all scientific and popular presentations of our day, modern man is considered to be the end of an unbroken stream of life by which he evolved from a single microscopic cell to the final stages. This belief in the evolution of man is an article in the creed of materialists and rationalists. Sir Arthur Keith stated this creed bluntly when he wrote, "A belief in evolution is a basal doctrine in the Rationalist liturgy."[1] Even the theistic evolutionist concedes the evolutionary origin of man from some prehuman form, who in turn evolved from an apelike ancestor. Some deny that evolution holds that man is descended from apes. But George Gaylord Simpson once pointed this out when he said that if anyone today were to encounter man's postulated Pliocene or Miocene ancestor, he would call him an ape.[2]

The Genesis account clearly points to a distinctive origin of man. From the beginning Adam and Eve were truly human individuals, created holy and with a complete knowledge of God (Col. 3:10; Eph. 2:24). They were real, historical persons. They were created by God in a particular manner and in a particular sequence from preexisting material—but not from preexisting life forms. This is attested to in both the Old and the New Testaments. It is a cornerstone of the Christian faith.

We have then two approaches to the problem of the origin of man, one evolutionary and the other creationist. The attempt to determine man's past has, unfortunately, been beclouded from both sides. On the one hand, some creationists have committed the sad error of refusing to accept bona fide fossils because they seemed to contradict, or pose apparently insoluble problems to, the creationist view of man's origin. It should be realized that where bones have been found as fossils they represent facts and must be dealt with as such. In addition, because some human paleontologists have been guilty of misrepresentation as well as honest mistakes, other creationists have tended to say, "A plague on your whole house" and have ignored all the findings of anthropology.

On the other hand, there has been a lack of objectivity and honesty on the part of some evolutionists and human paleontologists ranging from innocent error to, in some cases, outright fraud. A few examples will suffice. In 1922 Henry Fairfield Osborn of the American Museum hailed the unearthing of a tooth in Nebraska as the great discovery of the first American. He postulated a whole man and named him *Hesperopithecus,* considering him on a level with other "ape-men." It was even stated in interviews reported in newspapers that "William Jennings Bryan's Own State Speaks to Him on Evolution."[3] However, this tooth was later more accurately identified as the molar of a peccary (piglike) animal.

We have also Dubois' peculiar behavior over the *Pithecanthropus* finds (Java man). Dubois was the discoverer of the first *Pithecanthropus* remains. Although he publicized these in 1894, he concealed the fact that at the same time he had also found what later became known as the Wadjak skulls (Fig. A-3). The latter were kept under the floorboards of his room and were not made available to the public until 1920. Sir Arthur Keith excuses Dubois' action in these words. "There can be no doubt that if, on his [Dubois'] return in 1894, he had placed before the anthropologists of his time the ape-like skull from Trinil side by side with the great-brained skulls from Wadjak, both fossilized, both from the same region of Java, he would have given them a meal beyond the powers of their mental digestion."[4] Later Dubois kept the *Pithecanthropus* fragments in seclusion in his quarters, available for direct observation only through the glass of a bell jar. Even this opportunity was reserved only for a select few. Interestingly enough, toward the close of his life Dubois became convinced that his *Pithecanthropus* finds were not human at all, but rather the remains of a giant manlike ape possibly related to the gibbon.

At the other extreme we have the Piltdown forgery, a deliberate fraud, the author of which has still not been identified. Charles Dawson announced the finding of parts of a skull and lower jaw in gravel in Piltdown, Sussex. This was hailed as an important link in the evolution of ape to man. However, Kenneth Oakley demonstrated that the fluorine contents of the various pieces were different from those of other fossil bones found at the site. Later investigation also revealed that the teeth had been ground and altered to look more human. It is

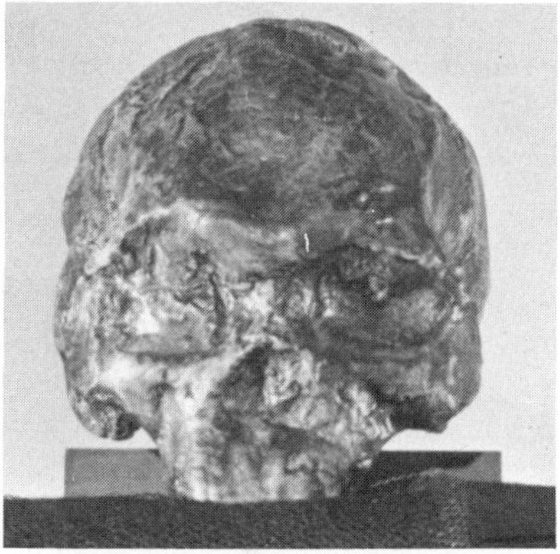

***Fig. A-3.* Wadjak skull from Java**

now agreed that the jaw is that of an ape. Francis Vere carefully considered the evidence and concluded that the fraud was intended as a hoax.[5] But Dr. W. R. Thompson points out that Sir Arthur Woodward, Charles Dawson, and Teilhard de Chardin, the only ones who might have carried out the fraud, were convinced and enthusiastic evolutionists. For these individuals, evolutionary doctrine was really a dogma. Hence Thompson doubts whether any of them would have made a practical joke about a matter so serious to them.[6] H. V. Vallois also supports this view, pointing out that he "sometimes wondered whether it was misguided impatience for the discovery of a more acceptable 'missing link' that formed one of the strands in the tangled skein of motives behind the Piltdown forgery (1912)."[7]

Dr. Himmelfarb wrote in 1959:

> Nor can it be maintained, as some Darwinians have done, that the exposure of Piltdown man leaves them no better and no worse off than they were before. It does, in fact, weaken their position in regard to both their theory and their methods. The zeal with which eminent scientists defended it, the facility with which even those who did not welcome it managed to accommodate themselves to it, and the way in which the most respected scientific techniques were soberly and painstakingly applied to it, with the apparent result of confirming both the genuineness of the fossils and the truth of evolution, are at the very least suspicious. However earnestly scientists may now dissociate themselves and their theory from Piltdown man, they cannot entirely wipe out the memory of forty years of labour expended on a deliberate and not particularly subtle fraud. And not forty years in the remote past, but forty years which came to an end only as recently as 1953.[8]

Finally, we are faced with a built-in bias against accepting any human fossils as genuine, if they turned up in too early a strata. This is pointed out by Broom and Schepers: "When someone produces relics of *Homo sapiens* in geological deposits more ancient than Mid-Pleistocene, we seek all manner of unlikely explanations for such an improbability, even going so far as to discredit usually reliable witnesses. Such finds ultimately become veritable skeletons in the cupboard to anthropologists, who, in the subconscious endeavors to support dogma, even fail to describe such finds fully enough to allow fools to enter where angels fear to tread."[9]

Therefore human fossils have been rejected solely on the basis that they were too modern for the strata in which they were found. Alois Hrdlicka of the Smithsonian Institution was known to have eliminated from serious consideration many human remains from collections of American museums he visited. He once wrote: "On the basis of what is positively known today in regard to early man and with the present scientific views regarding man's evolution, the anthropologist has a right to expect that human bones, particularly crania, exceeding a few thousand years in age, and more especially those of geological antiquity, shall point in the direction of more primitive forms." [10] Thus he branded as fraudulent any that were too "modern" for their location or level where found. Such was the weight of his authority that the specimen sometimes was then discarded. Evan Shute has compiled three pages of unaccepted human fossil finds, with the reasons why they were questioned. [11] In a number of instances their "modernity" is the sole basis for the questioning. (See also literature and later discussion on Fontchevade man.)

Finally I quote a recent statement by Dr. L. S. B. Leakey at Chicago: "We've had too many preconceived ideas and theories which, at the time they were formulated, were entirely justified on the basis of negative evidence. Theories are always desirable, but a certain number of them in recent years have been dressed up and have started to masquerade as facts, when they are not facts at all. And it is this that I am so seriously worried about—this disguising of theories as facts in textbooks and articles which means that we are shutting our eyes to the new knowledge." [12]

II. The Primates

The postulated line of man's descent follows from the earliest fossil primates through the entire Cenozoic era (the last of the four major geological eras). Zoologically, primates are considered to be mammals with a true placenta. They are more or less covered with a hairy or woolly coat. They have five fingers and five toes—the digits in most cases having flat nails instead of claws. The braincase is large and the brain is highly developed. The eyes are generally directed forward and are located in a socket surrounded by a ring of bone. The teeth, working from the center to the back, consist usually of two incisors on each side of each jaw, one canine tooth on each side of each jaw, two or three premolars on each side of each jaw, and finally three molars on each side of each jaw. The tooth arrangement for primates can be expressed in the form of a generalized dental formula, $\frac{1\text{-}2}{1\text{-}2} - \frac{0\text{-}1}{0\text{-}1} - \frac{1\text{-}3}{0\text{-}3} - \frac{2\text{-}3}{2\text{-}3}$, which indicates the tooth arrangement for both jaws on one side only since the other side is the same. The diet of primates is generally herbivorous, but may be omnivorous, or may consist entirely of insects. As a rule, only single offspring are produced at birth. Most primates are tree dwellers. Essentially they are a tropical and subtropical group. Examples can often be found in major zoological parks.

The order *Primates* is divided often into two suborders: the *Prosimii* and the *Simii.* (See Appendix A for the biological classification scheme; see Appendix B for George G. Simpson's proposed classification of the superfamily Hominoidea.) The prosimians do not look particularly monkey-like. See Fig. A-1. Technically they can be distinguished from the simians by the possession of a rhinarium, that is, the moist outer portion of the upper lip which runs from lip to nose. (This may be observed on any dog or cat.) Prosimians also have a frenulum, which is the membrane that anchors the upper lip to the upper jaw, preventing the upper lip from curling. The Prosimians are divided often into three infraorders: the *Lemuriformes;* the *Lorisiformes* (lorises and relatives); and the *Tarsiiformes* (tarsiers). The lemurs are about the size of a cat. They have a snout instead of a face, which gives them a somewhat foxlike appearance. Their fur is quite woolly. They have a long, bushy tail. They run on all four feet. Their generalized dental formula is $\frac{0\text{-}2}{1\text{-}2} - \frac{0\text{-}1}{0\text{-}1} - \frac{1\text{-}3}{0\text{-}3} - \frac{3}{3}$. The lorises are usually smaller bodied than the lemurs. They have a reduced second toe as well as a reduced index finger. They have larger eyes and ears and shorter tails. They move much more slowly and deliberately than do the lemurs. The dental formula of the lorises is $\frac{2}{2} - \frac{1}{1} - \frac{3}{3} - \frac{3}{3}$.

The tarsiers are found mainly in the Malay Peninsula and the Philippine Islands. They are called tarsiers because of the exceptional length of the tarsal part of the feet. The digits are often supplied with suctorial pads or discs. Tarsiers are about the size of rats. They are rather flat-faced with round heads, enormous eyes, and large ears. They can swivel their heads through a 180° turn. They are nocturnal animals, feeding mainly on insects. Their dental formula is $\frac{2}{1} - \frac{1}{1} - \frac{3}{3} - \frac{3}{3}$.

Figure A-1 **Prosimians**

A. A tarsier

B. Indri

C. Loris

D. Marmoset

Credits: **A.** tarsier, Larry Burrows, *Life* Magazine © Time Inc., **B.** indri, Terrence Spencer, *Life* Magazine © Time Inc.; **C.** loris, © Wolf Suschitzky, London; **D.** Marmoset, Nina Leen, *Life* Magazine © Time Inc.

The suborder *Simii* is also the *Anthropoidea* of many writers. This group contains the monkeys, apes, and man. The general characteristics seem to be the following: a bony bowl in back of the eye, as well as a bony ring around the eye (contrast with skull of dog or cat); the tear duct lying within the orbit of the eye; pectoral mammary glands; and the cerebrum (forebrain) overhanging the cerebellum (hind brain). This suborder is divided into three superfamilies: the *Ceboidea* or New World monkeys; the *Cercopithecoidea* or Old World monkeys; and the *Hominoidea,* the apes and man. The terms *Platyrrhini* and *Catarrhini,* often associated with these forms, are apparently falling into disuse.

The *Ceboidea* are divided into two families. The first, the *Callithricidae,* is composed of the marmosets. They are a primate exception, having nails only on the thumbs, with claws on the others. Their dental formula is $\frac{2}{2} - \frac{1}{1} - \frac{3}{3} - \frac{2}{2}$.

The larger family is the *Cebidae,* which consists of true monkeys. See Fig. A-2. They have nails on all digits. The New World monkeys are found in Central and South America. They are different in a number of ways from the Old World monkeys, notably in the possession of a long, strong tail which can be used for grasping branches to aid locomotion. They also have a wide space between their nostrils. They lack cheek pouches as well as the ischial callosities of the Old World monkeys. New World monkeys are four-footed limb crawlers and good brachiators, that is, they can swing from limb to limb of trees by their arms. Common examples are the Capuchins (organ grinder monkeys), Spider monkeys, Howler monkeys, etc. The dental formula for the Cebidae is $\frac{2}{2} - \frac{1}{1} - \frac{3}{3} - \frac{3}{3}$.

Ceropithecoidea are the Old World monkeys. Their nostrils are set close together. If they have tails, these are never used for grasping branches. Most of the *Ceropithecoidea* possess ischial callosities (bare, rough spots on which the animal sits). These are matched by a corresponding roughened area on the bone (ischium). The presence or absence of such a callosity can thus be inferred from fossil bones. Many also have cheek pouches. The chromosomal count ranges from 42 to 60. The

Old World monkeys are represented by such forms as the baboons, mandrills, rhesus monkeys, macaques, langurs, etc. Their dental formula is $\frac{2}{2}$ - $\frac{1}{1}$ - $\frac{2}{2}$ - $\frac{3}{3}$.

The third superfamily, the *Hominoidea,* lack tails and cheek pouches. Their dental formula is $\frac{2}{2}$ - $\frac{1}{1}$ - $\frac{2}{2}$ - $\frac{3}{3}$. Hominoidea are divided into three families: *Hylabatidae, Pongidae,* and *Hominidae. Hylabatidae* or gibbons live in the forests of southeast Asia. The height is usually less than 3 feet with a weight of 11 to 15 pounds. Their bodies are slender with long arms that reach to the toes. The gibbons are fantastic brachiators. Their diet is herbivorous, and they have long canines.

Pongidae or anthropoid apes include the living forms orangutan, gorilla, and chimpanzee. See Fig. A-2. The orangutan, confined to Borneo and Sumatra, lives mainly in trees, is herbivorous, and walks using its knuckles as well as its feet. It may reach a height in excess of 4 feet and a weight of about 165 pounds. Among the three great apes orangutans have the longest arms in proportion to other limbs. The male orangutan has a sagittal crest, that is, a ridge of bone running lengthwise across the top of the skull, as well as a transverse crest at the rear. The gorillas, confined to central western Africa, live in trees and are omnivorous in diet. They use the back of the hands to speed their locomotion. They may reach a height of 5–6 feet with a weight of 400 pounds. The 500–900 pound weight of zoo specimens is the result of obesity because of easy living and the lack of exercise in a cage. Also the male gorilla has a sagittal crest.

The chimpanzees are natives of western Africa. They are somewhat shorter and considerably lighter versions of the gorilla. They may reach a height of 5–5½ feet with a weight of about 110 pounds. "Chimps," in contrast to gorillas, lack the sagittal crest. The lips are long, very mobile, and protrusible. The face is rather nude. They have the most highly organized brain among animals. Their cranial capacity is 400 cc. They walk using the backs of their fingers. Chimpanzees have large projecting ears, which on sight distinguish them from gorillas.

Figure A-2

A. Woolly monkey

B. Male baboon

C. Gibbon

D. Orangutan

Credits: **A.** Woolly monkey and **B.** male baboon © Time Inc.; **C.** gibbon, Nina Leen, *Life* Magazine © Time Inc.; **D.** orangutan, courtesy of the American Museum of Natural History

III. The Hominidae

The third family is the *Hominidae,* containing a single genus, with a single living species, *Homo sapiens* or modern man. Man has been defined as being a big-brained primate with the power of speech, who makes and uses tools. His face is relatively small compared to brain vault. Man is the only mammal with *permanent* bipedal locomotion, whereas apes are usually quadrapedal, walking on their hind feet and the knuckles of their hands. The human nose has a prominent bridge and elongated tip, whereas apes have noses that are flat in root and bridge. The human lip has a median furrow and is controlled so the mucous lining shows a red line. A comparison of man and the apes is given in tabular form in Table I.

Table I

	Modern Man	***Apes***
1.	Large vaulted cranium	Flattened cranium
2.	Mastoid process prominent (See Fig. I, A1)	Mastoid process absent or inconspicuous
3.	Dental arch parabolic (See Fig. I, C2)	Dental arch U-shaped (See Fig. I, D2)
4.	Canines project little, if at all	Projecting canines
5.	No diastema in upper jaw (See Fig. I, C1)	Diastema present (See Fig. I, D1)
6.	No simian shelf	Simian shelf (See Fig. I)
*7.	Lips prominent	Lips extremely thin
8.	Vertebral column in 3 curves	Vertebral column in 2 curves
9.	Short neural spines on cervical vertebrae	Long neural spines on cervical vertebrae
10.	Relatively short arms	Relatively long arms
*11.	Lower placed nipples	Higher placed nipples
*12.	Female with persistent breasts	Female with flattened breasts
*13.	Body relatively hairless	Body relatively hairy
*14.	Body hair, when present, most prominent on ventral (belly) body surface	Body hair always present, most prominent on dorsal (back) surface
15.	No baculum (os penis)	Baculum present (os penis)
16.	Deep, bowl-shaped pelvis (See Fig. II - B)	Shallow, flattened pelvis (See Fig. II - D)
*17.	Bulging gluteus maximus (buttocks)	Flattened gluteus maximus
18.	Linea aspara present on femur (ridge for muscle attachment)	Linea aspara absent
19.	Feet different from hands (See Fig. III)	Feet similar to hands

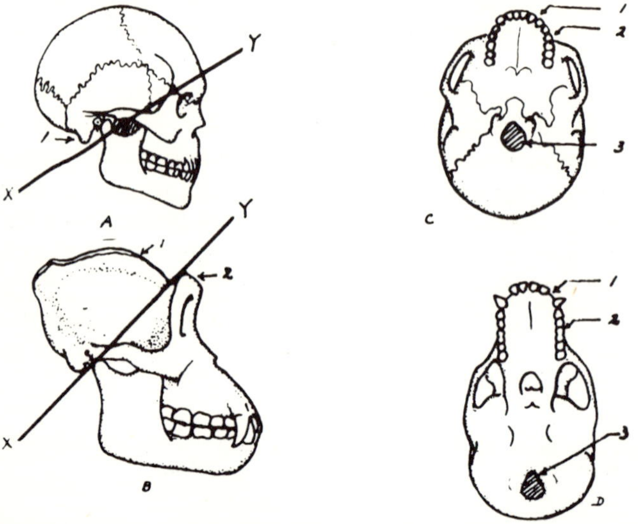

Fig. I. Comparison between the skulls of male gorilla and man. A. Side view of skull of man. B. Side view of skull of gorilla. C. Bottom view of skull of man. D. Bottom view of skull of gorilla. Line X-Y illustrates face to brain-case ratio.

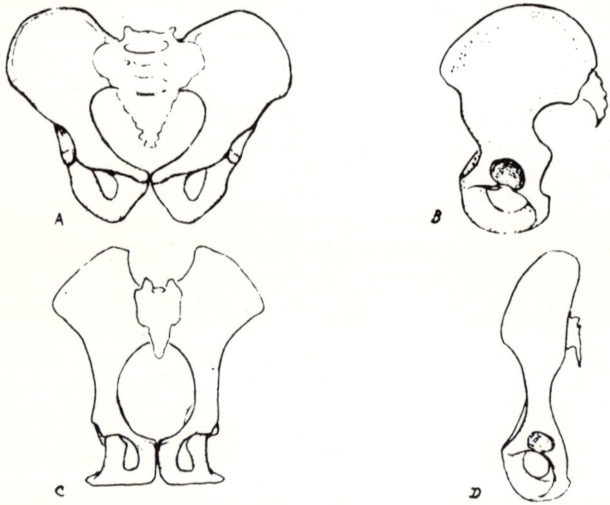

Fig. II. Pelvis of man compared to that of gorilla. A. Frontal view of human pelvis. B. Lateral view of human pelvis. C. Frontal view of gorilla pelvis. D. Lateral view of gorilla pelvis.

Fig. III. Foot of man compared to that of ape.

Biegert, J., *Volarhaut der Hände und Füsse.* Primatologia II/I, Lieferung 3, (Basel: S. Karger, 1961).

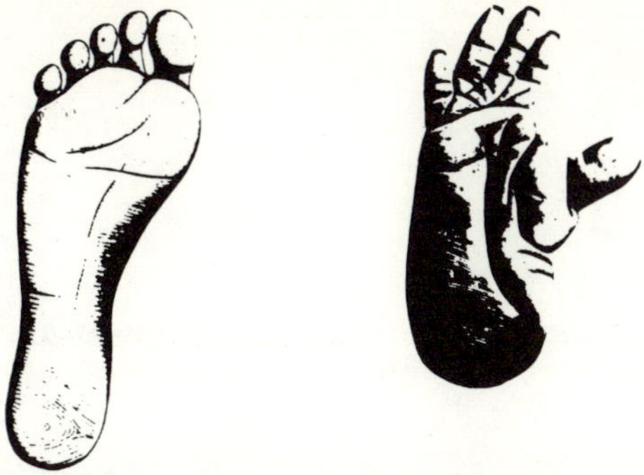

* The items marked in Table I with an asterisk, the fleshy items in the paragraph preceding the table, as well as behavior patterns and physiology are not subject to fossilization. After death and decay, all that remains are hard parts, such as bones and teeth which may or may not become fossilized. Therefore, full skeletal remains are rare, in which cases many of the hard parts mentioned (i. e., baculum, lower jaws, etc.) may not be part of the find. In anthropological works men speak of their discoveries with a great deal of certainty and detail, but it should be remembered that their discoveries are almost never whole skeletons. Instead they are usually partial skeletons without trunks or limbs, many are faceless, and quite a few are represented only by a few teeth and jaw fragments.

Man exceeds both monkeys and apes in the early growth of the lower limbs. Man's head grows narrower in proportion to its length, but the heads of monkeys and apes retain a constant proportion or grow broader. The jaws, which lie largely below the cranium at birth, grow forward to jut out in adult life. In chimps and gorillas the eye orbits move forward from beneath the brain to end up in front of it. Man's dentition is such that he can grind the lower against the upper teeth, from side to side and from front to back. Apes simply compress the jaws up and down. The teeth of both fossil men and living primitives are often worn flat from chewing, whereas those of apes, because of their chewing method, do not show much

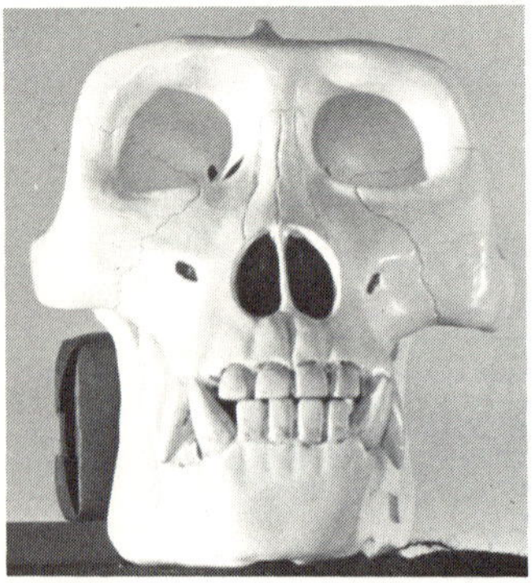

A.

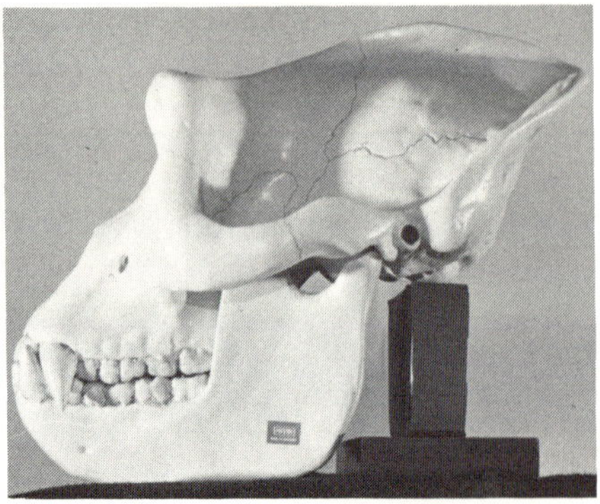

B.

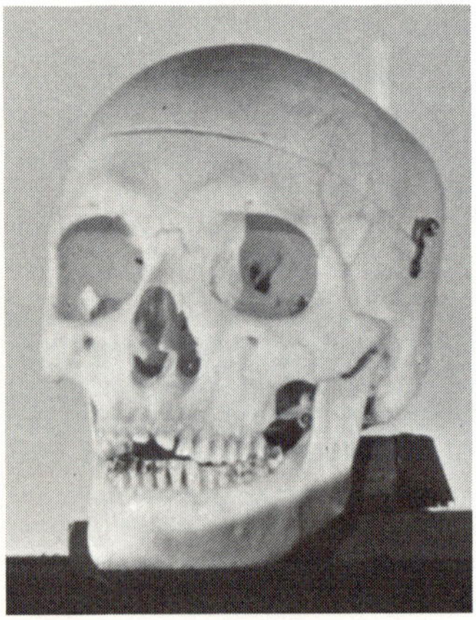

C.

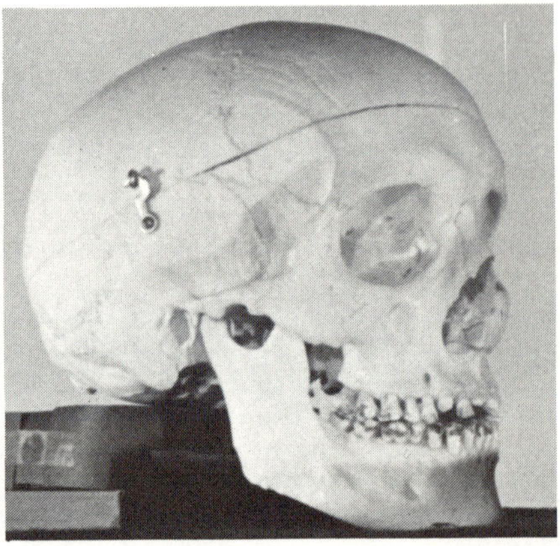

D.

Fig. A-4. Comparisons between human and gorilla skulls. Frontal view (a) and profile view (b) of skull of male gorilla. Frontal view (c) and diagonal view (d) of human skull (Sikh?).

wear. The acetabulum or hip socket is very shallow in apes, while it is deep in man. The femur in man is longer, stronger and thicker, and has a ridge, the linea aspara, for the attachment of thigh and buttock muscles. Apes lacking the linea aspara therefore do not have the rounded thighs and projecting buttocks of normal humans.

All of these characteristics are related to the fact that standing erect continuously and true walking are peculiarly human abilities. Apes run bipedally to keep from falling forward, but they can stand erect without moving only a very short time. Usually apes travel using the knuckles of the front arms in addition to the hind limbs. Man has a longer neck than apes; the neck of apes is short and not very mobile. Dr. F. G. Parsons wrote, "A greater gap exists between the musculature of man and that of other Primates than there is between many different orders." [13]

Men and apes can be compared, as Cuvier did, on the basis of the ratio between the cranial capacity and the size of the face. Man has the largest cranium and the smallest face, proportionately, of all the primates. Cf. Fig. I. However, cranium size, which means brain volume, is not a reliable criterion for determining intelligence. This is evident when one considers that a brain volume of 800 to 2,200 cc. (cubic centimeters) is regarded as a normal range for modern man. Anatole France, one of the great French men of letters, is reported to have had a brain volume of 1,017 cc. or 1,100 cc., and yet this figure is well within the range of Pithecanthropus forms. On the other hand, Jonathan Swift had a brain volume close to 2,000 cc. Who is to say which of these two men was the more intelligent?

Sir James Gray, F. R. S., Cambridge University, stated: "It would be very convenient if step by step with an increase in size and complexity of the brain it were possible to trace a corresponding increase in complexity of behavior and ability to learn. Unfortunately this is not the case." [14] It should also be remembered that the average brain volume for Neanderthal man, on the basis of all known classic finds, is greater than the average for modern man, although the upper and lower limits for modern man are greater. How did Neanderthal compare with modern man with respect to intelligence?

In this respect Sir Francis Walshe once reflected on the equation of mind with brain. He read a monograph on the cerebral cortex of man which stated the following: "If the proper study of mankind is man, surely the supreme biological interest of man is his brain, particularly the grey cortex of two billion cells, without the orchestration of which there can be no thought, no sweet sonnets of Shakespeare, no joy and no sorrow." To this Walshe replied: "What a typical materialist half-truth! What a pregnant silence about the other half, for, from the dumbest blonde to the wisest sage, each of us has a quota of two billion grey cells, yet the human race has produced but one Shakespeare." [15]

Although man is a mammal and his structure and anatomy have many similarities to those of the anthropoid apes, a knowledge of the structure and anatomy of man (much less that of just partial fossil remains) is not sufficient to enable us to correctly appraise his life and appearance or his status in the world of his day. Any organism is something more than the sum total of its flesh, secretions, and skeletal parts.

But just wherein really lie the differences between man and animals? That man was created in the image of God and given a soul and spirit would seem to be the fundamental difference that the Bible makes between man and the rest of the animal kingdom. Prior to the Fall, the image of God also consisted of true righteousness and holiness (Eph. 4:24; Col. 3:10). Genesis says man was created in the image of God (Gen. 1:27). Does *imago Dei* mean a physical resemblance? Manifestly this would be absurd, and there is no indication that Scripture teaches that such a resemblance is meant.

The writer of Ecclesiastes certainly recognizes the physical and physiological relationship of man with the animals when he states: "I said in my heart with regard to the sons of men that God is testing them to show them that they are but beasts. For the fate of the sons of men and the fate of beasts is the same; as one dies, so dies the other. They all have the same breath, and man has no advantage over the beasts; for all is vanity. All go to one place, all are from the dust, and all turn to dust." Eccl. 3:18-20 (RSV). Yet in verse 21 he points out the psychic differences between man and the animals:

"Who knoweth the spirit of man that goeth upward and the spirit of the beast that goeth downward to the earth?" (KJV). And again in Eccl. 12:7: "and the spirit [of man] shall return unto God who gave it."

The human paleontologist uses the evidence of fire and tool-making to determine humanity. He asks the question, "Are there or are there not tools associated with the skeletal remains?" The presence of ashes and charcoal indicates the controlled use of fire. Recent observations of primate behavior made by various investigators, such as Jane Goodall, have indicated that chimpanzees crush leaves and use them as a sponge to soak up water from a cavity. But this is not the use of a tool in the strict sense, as using a stone to fashion another tool such as a point. It is this latter type of tool-making that is distinctively and consistently human. These are the criteria of humanity for the paleontologist.

From the anthropological viewpoint, it might be said that man is distinguished from the animals by his possession of culture. Carleton Coon once said: "Culture is the sum total of things that a people do as a result of having been so taught." [16] R. Linton wrote that culture is "an organized group of learned responses characteristic of a particular society." [17]

Man is born with a minimum of behavior patterns, and must learn social behavior after birth. Therefore he may and does vary all over the face of the globe in this respect. Man could not mature in isolation. Where would he learn his behavior patterns? If an Eskimo infant and a Zulu infant were interchanged, each would grow up speaking the language and following the culture pattern of their new environment.

How and whence could human culture arise of itself? In this matter of culture, there is a tremendous gap between man and animals. Sahlins asserts that "there is quantum difference, at points a complete opposition, between even the most rudimentary human society and the most advanced subhuman one. The discontinuity implies that the emergence of human society required some suppression, rather than a direct expression of man's primate nature." [18] Loren Eisely implied the same when he wrote, "What must have been the frightening withdrawal of instinct in man and its replacement by the culture-building brain is a passage that the Darwinian world failed to grasp or appreciate clearly."[19]

Finally note the opinion of Hebb and Thompson. "Man has what neither chimpanzee nor parrot has: the capacity to combine and readily recombine representative or symbolic noises (words), movements (gestures), or modifications of inert things (writing, carving). We propose therefore that the minimal criterion of language as distinct from other purposive communication, is twofold. First, language combines two or more representative gestures or noises purposefully for a single effect; and secondly, it uses the same gestures in different combinations for different effects, changing readily with circumstances."[20]

IV. The Fossil Record

What has been the line of man's descent postulated by the proponents of his evolutionary origin? Ideas have been many and varied. Douglas Dewar summarized those that have been proposed from the time of Darwin to recent times in his *The Transformist Illusion.*[21] (See Appendix C.) As one can see from Dewar's presentation, there is quite an array with wide disagreements. The variations are possible because of a lack of evidence for any one certain derivation.

To follow the discussion of human fossils, one should be familiar with the terminology used in the following part of the geologic time scale.

Cenozoic Era	Quaternary Period	Recent Epoch 10,000 years	3 my*
		Pleistocene Epoch 1–3 my	
		Pliocene Epoch 12–14 my	
		Miocene Epoch 12–13 my	
	Tertiary Period	Oligocene Epoch 11–14 my	66 my
		Eocene Epoch 20–22 my	
		Paleocene Epoch 5–10 my	

* million years

In addition one should be familiar with the usual subdivisions of the Pleistocene. This is broken up into four glacial episodes separated by interglacials as follows:

American geological usage	European and anthropological equivalent
Wisconsin glaciation	Würm
Sangamon interglacial	Würm–Riss
Illinoisan glaciation	Riss
Yarmouth interglacial	Riss–Mindel
Kansan glaciation	Mindel
Aftonian interglacial	Mindel–Günz
Nebraskan glaciation	Günz

Human fossil finds seem to be confined to strata considered to be of Pleistocene or, at the earliest, Pliocene age.

The geologist works with rock units; the basic one is the formation. This is usually given two names; the first is geographic, having the name of the locality where it was first identified and described. The second name refers to the rock type, such as sandstone, shale, limestone, etc., provided the formation is composed of a single type of sediment. Thus a formation which is rich in dinosaur fossils in the western part of our country is called the Morrison formation. A prominent hogback formation on the east slope of the Rockies is the Dakota sandstone.

The paleontologist may refer to the Pliocene epoch as a time period, or to rocks of Pliocene age, that is, a set of rocks deposited during Pliocene time. He might also refer to a given formation, such as the Djetis bed in Java (locality of the Modjokerto infant) or Mauer sands (site of Heidelberg jaw) in Germany or the Thasbech Travertine (locality of the Taung skull). Most human fossil sites are dated on the basis of associated mammalian remains, such as mammoths, primitive oxen, sabre-toothed cats, etc. Today potassium-argon dating is often used to ascertain the ages of the deposit—necessarily by determining the age of the overlying or underlying deposits.

Let it be understood that the writer uses the names of the geological epochs in the following discussion to indicate possible *relative* dating, without necessarily accepting the usual geological time estimates.

It is in the Paleocene beds of Wyoming that the first primate fossils in the Americas turned up in a great primate explosion. Then they ceased to appear, and no more primate fossils are known in the Americas until human fossils appeared in relatively recent deposits. All the American and European finds so far are of fossil prosimians belonging to genera that have either died out or have close affinities to present-day lemurs and tarsiers. In the Oligocene beds of Fayum, Egypt, small primate fossils of forms resembling lemurs are found. They consist of fragments of mandibles and teeth. It is strange from the point of view of the evolutionist that there are no Paleozoic or Eocene fossil primates found in any part of the African continent. In fact there are none prior to the Miocene in central or southern Africa. Some have noted this fact with astonishment, since this is the area considered by many to be the cradle of man's development.[22]

George G. Simpson remarks that "no Anthropoidea have yet been definitely identified before early Oligocene."[23]

In the south of France in 1856 a jawbone of *Dryopithecus* was discovered in Miocene beds. Eduard Lartet and Albert Gaudry at first hailed it as being closer to man than any other monkey. However, a more complete and better preserved jawbone turned up in 1890, and Gaudry then admitted that this fossil monkey resembled man less than the living anthropoids. In 1935 G. E. Lewis located fragments of jaw and teeth in the upper Miocene strata of the Siwalik Hills in India.[24] This find was again hailed by Lewis as resembling man more than any other known monkey.

A large ape, *Proconsul,* was discovered by L. S. B. Leakey in Africa. There has been considerable disagreement as to whether this form should be considered in the line of man's ancestor or not. The lower jaw lacks a simian shelf.[25] However, it is considered today that *Proconsul* closely relates to the dog-faced monkeys (*Cynomorpha*). There is some doubt, also, as to whether it had stereoscopic vision, since the eye sockets face slightly to each side.

Finally mention should be made of *Oreopithecus bambolii.* This fossil was discovered when, after lengthy use of a coal mine near Monte Bamboli in Italy, someone finally happened to observe a complete skeleton imbedded in the roof slab. Although there was considerable debate as to its position in the scheme of human evolution, this fossil from the upper

Miocene is now also considered a cynomorph by many human paleontologists. Others include this form among the anthropoid apes (see Appendix C). All of these forms have been considered to be "common ancestral" forms of man at various times. However the evidence is far from conclusive. In the case of the fossil primates previously discussed, other than *Oreopithecus bambolii,* no complete skeleton is known. The fossil remains of primates other than man are so fragmentary that they cast little light on supposed evolutionary lines of descent. In most instances the finds consist of little more than jaw fragments and teeth. Thus many admit that the gap between hominid and anthropoid is not yet filled.

It is worthwhile spending a little more time on *Dryopithecus* and related forms. At one time many new tooth and jaw finds called for the establishment of a new genus, until there were a grand total of 26! An example of one of these forms is *Sivapithecus indicus.* The illustration shows what is known of this fossil (see Fig. A-5). Today, after reexamination of the more than 500 fossil fragments, these 26 genera have been reduced to three: *Dryopithecus* (Fig. A-5), *Gigantopithecus,* and *Ramapithecus. Kenyapithecus* is included in the latter. The first two genera are now classed as *Pongidae,* while the last one is classed as *Hominidae.* For some time there were two separate genera: *Ramapithecus,* consisting of upper-jaw fragments, and *Bramapithecus* consisting of lower-jaw fragments. The names indicate that these were found in India. It was later demonstrated that the upper fragments of *Bramapithecus* and the lower fragments of *Ramapithecus* fit together—and so two genera became one, *Ramapithecus.* On the basis of a smaller canine, and a reconstruction showing an arch more like man's, this Miocene form has been pronounced by many to be an ancestral form of *Homo.*[26] However, it should be remembered that those parts of the skeleton, such as the skull and extremities, that distinguish apes from men are still unknown. Hence any definite classification as ape or hominid is premature to say the least.

The first fossil forms generally agreed to be humanoid appear in the Pliocene. However, it is necessary to further explain terminology before discussing these forms. A confusing factor in physical anthropology is the habit of assigning each

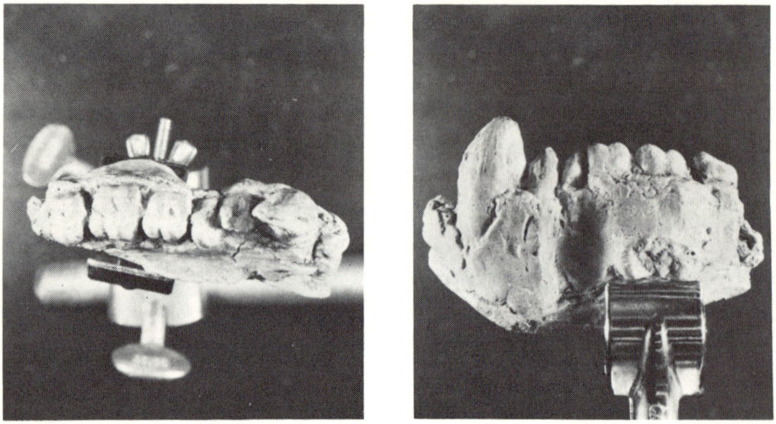

A. Top

B. Outside

Fig. A-5. Top and outside (buccal) view of mandible fragment of *Sivapithecus (Dryopithecus) indicus.*

new find to its own genus. The process is described by Prof. H. H. Woolland. "When a new fossil has been discovered, the discoverer has been unable to resist the temptation of asserting that his fossil, if ape-like, presented all sorts of human characters, and if human and clearly modern in character, it possessed all sorts of simian characters, more or less hidden and elucidated only by minute examination."[27]

Others have recognized that anthropologists have been multiplying genera needlessly. Theodosious Dobzhansky referred to such multiplication when he wrote that "a minor but rather amazing difficulty for a biologist is the habit human paleontologists have of flattering their egos by naming each find a new species, if not a new genus. This causes not only needless cluttering of the nomenclature, but it is seriously misleading because treating as a species what is not a species beclouds some important issues."[28] George G. Simpson was even harsher when he wrote, "Insofar as the chaos is due to faulty linguistics rather than to zoological disagreements, it stems either from ignorance or from refusal to follow rules and usages.

This must be almost the only field in science in which those who do not know and follow the established norms have so frequently had the temerity and opportunity to publish research that is, in this respect, incompetent."[29]

There is now a tendency among anthropologists to rectify these matters. The present situation in taxonomy seems to be the following:

Modern man—*Homo sapiens sapiens*

Cro-Magnon man—*Homo sapiens sapiens*

All Neanderthal forms—*Homo sapiens neanderthalensis*

All Neanderthaloid forms—*Homo sapiens*

Pithecanthropine forms—*Homo erectus erectus*

At the National Academy of Science meeting, Washington, Oct. 16, 1965, all nonhominids were included in one genus, *Australopithecus* with two species, *africanus* and *robustus. Paranthropus* was placed into the latter species. Along these lines, Carleton Coon has given an excellent discussion in his *Origin of Races.* His final conclusion is: "The concept that the fossil men so far found, who lived during the last half million years, belonged to more than one genus is impossible, both anatomically and in terms of behavior as revealed by archaeology. This concept must be abandoned, and indeed, many zoologists and anthropologists have already discarded it. Of the names proposed for our genus, *Homo* has two centuries of priority, and *Homo* is what we are, what our known ancestors were, and what our unknown ancestors could have been for as long as eight million years."[30]

V. The Neanderthals

At this point let us examine the human fossil record itself. One of the earliest validated human fossils was discovered in 1856 in a cave in the Neanderthal Valley of the River Düssel. At the time not much was made of this discovery. Later, in 1864, at a meeting of the Royal Zoological Society of London an English geologist, G. Burk, showed a human skull that had been excavated in 1846 in Gibraltar. This skull was compared with the Neanderthal skull. The similarities were noted, after which the matter seems to have been forgotten. Then in 1866 the "man of Spy" was discovered. Actually three skeletons were found, but none were complete. It was not until 1908 that the complete skeleton of a man similar to the previous finds was discovered at La Chapelle-aux-Saints in France. (See Fig. A-6.)

Studies of these skeletons indicated a number of differences between them and the skeleton of modern man. However, the volume range of Neanderthal skulls, 1,300 to 1,600 cc., falls within the range of that of modern man, whose skull volume ranges from ca. 1,000 to 1,900 cc. In our time no competent anthropologist considers the brain of Neanderthal to have been inferior to that of modern man in any way. The face is larger than that of modern man. The outstanding differentiating characteristics of the Neanderthal skull are the bun-shaped occipital region, the generally broader lower part of the skull, the postorbital constrictions, the supraorbital ridges, and the lack of consistent mental protuberance (chin). Today it is generally known that osteoarthritis was a common affliction of Neanderthal man. He has therefore been erroneously but popularly portrayed as hunch-backed, with shuffling feet. Nevertheless, he could (when healthy) have stood as erect as any modern man.

In dealing with actual fossil evidence, it is well to remember that reconstructions are not the exact scientifically objective things that they are purported to be. The case of Neanderthal man and the previous quotation of Dr. H. H. Woolland support this opinion. In addition, one may page through historical geology books and note the differences in appearance of the various reconstructions of *Tyrannosaurus rex,* the cycle of *Stegosaurus* reconstructions through the years, as well as the differences from text to text. Note also the varied facial reconstructions of various noted human fossil finds. See Fig. A-7. Even though the paleontologist regularly engages in reconstructions himself, he is bothered by the anthropologist's comprehensive conclusions based on a small amount of data. Dr. Glen Jepsen recently remarked that "we need more specimens. We have many competent anthropologists, what we need is more competent fossils."[31] This statement does not imply that there was any doubt in the mind of the speaker that man has evolved.

Neanderthal man was apparently widely distributed and is especially well known in Southern Russia, where his

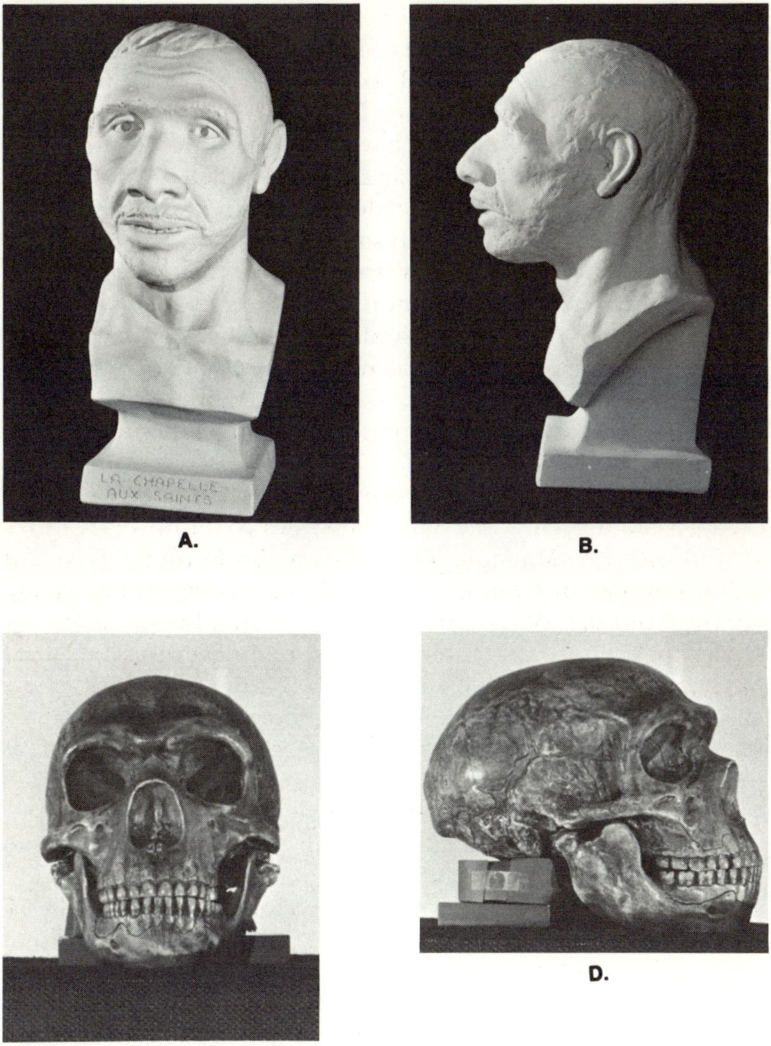

A. B. C. D.

Fig. A-6. Front (A) and profile (B) views of flesh reconstruction of La Chapelle-aux-Saints Neanderthal find. Front (C) and profile (D) view of reconstructed skull of La Chapelle.

clustered dwellings have been discovered.[32] In this region Neanderthal man built shelters of mammoth tusks and ribs and covered them with hides and earth.[33] Primitive religious ceremonies may have been celebrated by Neanderthal man. Blanc discovered a Neanderthal skull in a cave in Monte Circeo, Italy, which had been placed in the center of a cleared area surrounded by a circle of cave bear and cave hyena bones.[34]

Neanderthal skeletons have also been found in La Ferrassie, La Moustier, La Quina, and La Naulette, France; and Sacco-Pastore, Italy. Neanderthal remains have also been found in Shanidar Cave in Iran. At the time the discoveries were made, the cave was still occupied. So the caveman's way of life continues in our present day.

The most important findings relating to Neanderthal man are those reported by McCown and Keith in 1939.[35] These were discovered in two caves: Skhul and Tabun in the Mount Carmel area in Palestine. All represent deliberate burials. The range in form from Skhul V to Tabun I was found to be unexpectedly great. Tabun possesses features which link it to the classic Neanderthal, while Skhul possesses Neanthropic features shared with Cro-Magnon. Yet McCown and Keith held that the Skhul population from that cave was antecedent to the Tabun people from the 'B' layer in that cave, but also being contemporary with Tabun I and Tabun II from a lower level. These finds have caused considerable controversy. Many now consider the existence of a pre-Neanderthal form, more resembling modern man, which was antecedent to the classic Neanderthal as previously described. Such modern appearing pre-Neanderthals are usually referred to as Neanderthaloids.

The Neanderthaloids differ from the classic Neanderthals in having higher skull vaults and a more modern lower jaw, showing varying amounts of chin development (see Fig. A-7). Among these Neanderthaloid forms, also often referred to as pre-Mousterian Man, many would place the Shanidar form previously referred to; Rhodesian Man from Broken Hill; the skull found at Saldanba Bay, 90 miles north of Capetown, South Africa; the Java finds at Ngandang on the River Solo, consisting of 11 skulls comprising what is referred to as Solo Man; Krapina Man; and others. Neanderthaloids would still be classed *Homo sapiens*.

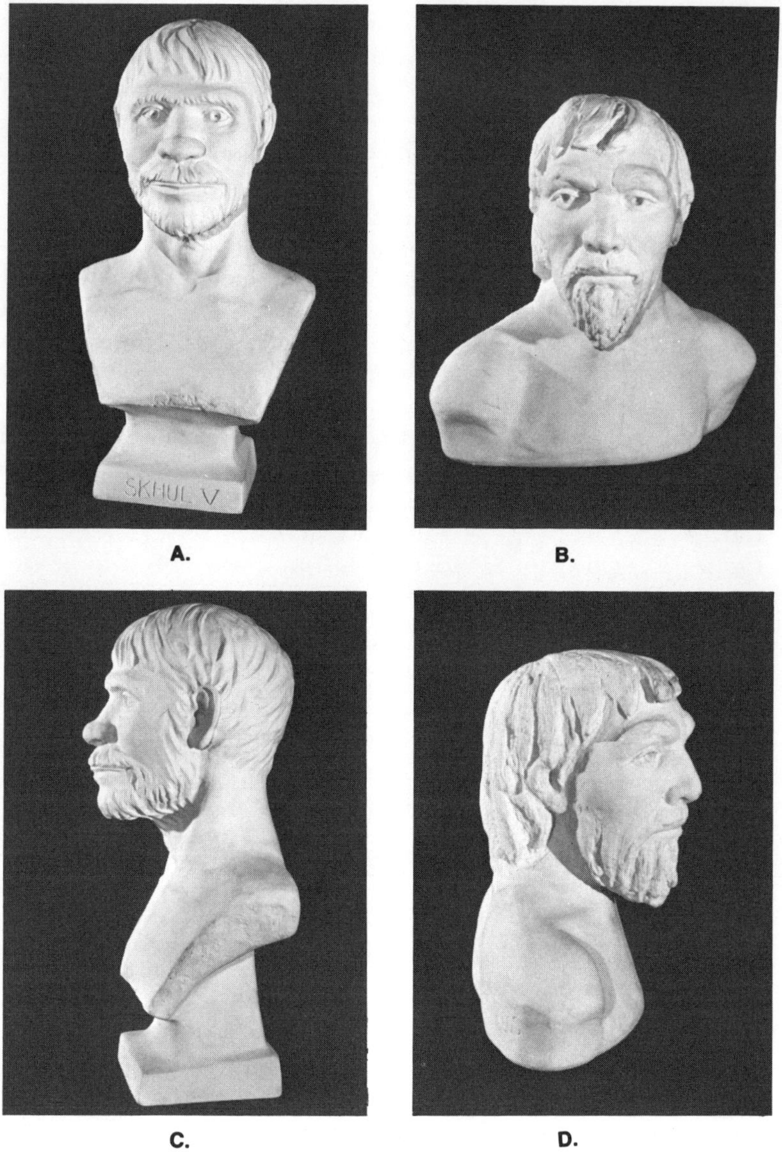

Fig. A-7. Frontal (A) and side (C) views of a flesh reproduction of Skhul V by Maurice P. Coon. Frontal (B) and side (D) views of a flesh reproduction of the *same* skull by Stephen Beames.

In the summer of 1947 Germaine Henri-Martin found two fossil skulls, one possibly of a woman, in a cave of Fontechevade, Charent, France.[36] The bones apparently are in no way outside the range of *Homo sapiens.* They were found *in situ,* in a horizon covered with a thick layer of dripstone which indicated a considerable time gap between the two layers. The Mousterian culture lies above this dripstone. The find therefore has been ranked with the Swanscombe fossil as evidence for an early existence of *Homo sapiens.* L. Eisely says the skull is that of a modern woman.[37] This supports the prophetic opinion of J. Kälin who had suggested that this skull indicates that Neanderthal man has lost some of the modern features that were in existence prior to him. It may be concluded that since modern types lived simultaneously with classical Neanderthal forms, Neanderthal certainly cannot be a stage in the evolution of modern man. Many anthropologists hold that classical Neanderthal represents a separate, essentially terminal line of human variation and development.[38 *to* 40]

A parallel situation has been observed in Aleutian fossils in Alaska. William Laughlin describes findings there which show that the paleo-Aleuts were less primitive in skull appearance than the neo-Aleuts. The change probably occurred in a relatively short period of time, probably something like 4,000 years.[41] The variation from paleo-Aleut to neo-Aleut involved a broadening and corresponding flattening of the skull reminiscent of the change from modern man to Neanderthal. Laughlin considers this variation to be an adaptation to a colder environment.

VI. The Pithecanthropines

Having evaluated the present status of *Homo sapiens neanderthalensis,* let us examine the *Homo erectus* forms. This form was discovered by Dr. Eugene Dubois, a Dutch army surgeon who went to Java in 1889, determined to find the "missing link." In 1894 he returned to Holland with 215 packing cases of fossils. Prior to his departure he published a paper in Batavia entitled "Pithecanthropus Erectus, a Transition Form from Java."[42] He described his finds as a skull cap, a thigh bone, and jaw fragments subsequently known as *Pithecanthropus*

I (H. erectus pithecanthropus). In 1895 he appeared before the Third International Congress of Zoologists at Leyden showing his fossils and describing their discovery. Doubt was expressed as to whether these necessarily all came from the same individual. Virchow, the great anatomist, was one of the doubters. A later expedition to the Dubois site in 1906 was led by Frau Lenore Selenka.[43] Selenka moved large quantities of earth and found many fossils, but no more specimens of *Pithecanthropus.* She also reported that *Pithecanthropus* was found in mid-Pleistocene deposits, rather than the Pliocene, as Dubois had maintained. This had the effect of decreasing the estimated age of the Java man.

In 1920 Dubois exhibited his big-brained finds, the Wadjak skulls (see Fig. A-3), and in 1924 he also produced a lower jaw he had found in Java in 1890, as well as some thigh bones. At that time he reported to the Royal Society at Amsterdam that *Pithecanthropus,* in his opinion, was a definite hominid. At a later date a fluorine test of the skulls and the femurs showed identical fluorine content, indicating that both came from the same population.[44]

Dubois' Wadjak skulls have exceptionally large cranial capacities, skull I being 1,550 cc. while skull II is 1,650 cc. The jaws were described by Dubois as being as massive as those of Heidelberg man. Since then they have been considered to be Proto-Australian. Carleton Coon considers them to be full members of *Homo sapiens,* but still notes resemblances between them and *Pithecanthropus.*[45]

G. H. R. von Königswald was intrigued to such an extent by the skull cap of *Pithecanthropus* that he went to Java himself in search of more fossils. He found the jawbone of Sangiran, which has been attributed to *Pithecanthropus,* a skull cap; *Pithecanthropus II,* which is almost an exact duplicate of Dubois' find; a right parietal bone with parts of left parietal and occipital bones which form what is called *Pithecanthropus IV.* However, all the Java *Pithecanthropus* remains do not add up to a complete skull. Nose and cheek regions as well as the vertical ramus of the lower jaw are still unknown. They have been reconstructed using *Sinanthropus (H. erectus pekinsis*—Peking man) as the model.

The alleged evolutionary picture is complicated by the further discoveries of von Königswald. In 1936, at Modjokerto, near Surabaya, Java, he found the skull of a young child, which has been called the Modjokerto child. This form must be older than *Pithecanthropus,* since it occurs in the Djetis level, which is considered to be older than the Trinil levels in which *Pithecanthropus* is found. A number of modern characteristics such as a rounded occipital bone, larger parietal area than frontal, and a deep mastoid fossa have caused great debate. The face is missing. Von Königswald also discovered a lower jawbone fragment larger than any modern or fossil human jaw as well as that of most anthropoid apes. The teeth are also gigantic, but they are distinctly human. Von Königswald originally named this find *Meganthropus,* but later named it *Pithecanthropus dubius.*[46] Le Gros Clark holds it is *Homo erectus.*[47] Robinson, on the other hand, considers *Meganthropus* to be an Australopithecine.[48]

Apothecary shops in China have been very fruitful hunting for paleontologists. Such teeth are known as "dragon's teeth" by the Chinese, and were considered to be useful for medicinal purposes. Von Königswald searched for and found many of these. Some were sent to F. Weidenreich at the American Museum of Natural History. Among several large orang *Stegodon* and tapir teeth were three human teeth which were six times as large as normal. Von Königswald called them representative of *Giganthropithecus.* Weidenreich said they came from a form that should be called *Gigantanthropus.* Thus one scientist thought they were from a giant ape; the other believed them to be from a giant man.

Certainly these large teeth pose a problem. From what kind of human (if human they were) did they come? Weidenreich was fond of using the Genesis reference, "and there were giants in those days" (Gen. 6:4). These teeth formed the basis for his contention that modern man has descended from gigantic forebears. In any case the teeth remain a tantalizing puzzle. However, there is a tendency today to group them with *Meganthropus* as being of Australopithecine origin.

About this time a number of human bones, including a skull, were found 25 miles southwest of Pekin. This led to the

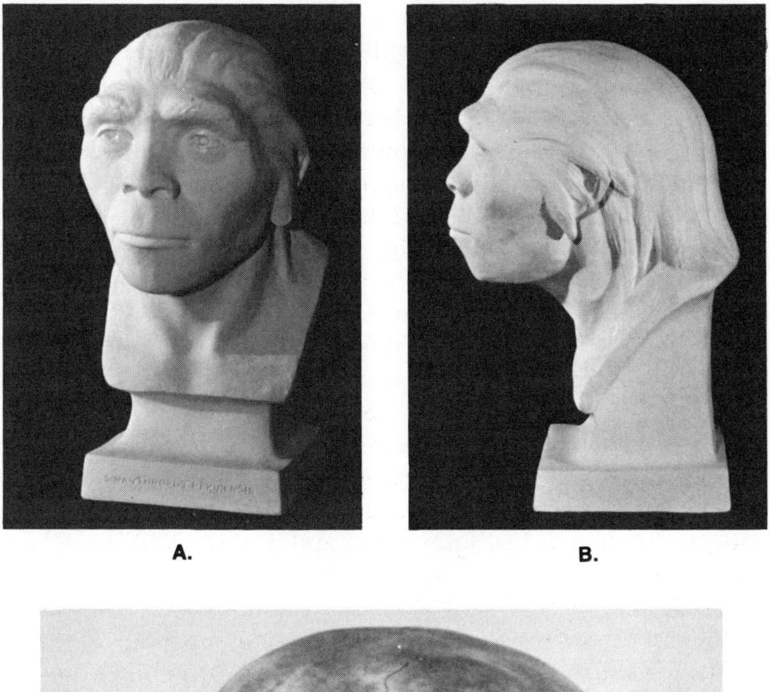

A. B. C.

Fig. A-8. Frontal (A) and profile (B) views of flesh reconstruction of *Sinanthropus*. Profile (C) view of Weidenreich's skull reconstruction.

systematic excavation of the site known as Chou-Kou-Tien (Chicken-bone Hill). The first discoverer of fossils in this area, Dr. Davidson Black, named the find *Sinanthropus pekinensis (H. erectus pekinensis*—Peking Man). See Fig. A-8. By the time excavations were finished, 38 individuals, including 15 children, had been uncovered. All of the fossils were more or less incomplete. The specimens indicated that Peking Man had a low forehead, a flat cranium, brow ridge, an occipital ridge at the nape, a projecting face, and long bones much like modern man's, far different from those of apes. In addition to the fossil remains, hearth ashes indicated the controlled use of fire. A stone and bone industry were also found. Le Gros Clark points out that some of the cranial capacities come well within the normal range of modern man, and the limb bones do not appear to differ from those of *Homo sapiens.* These discoveries force the conclusion that *Sinanthropus* was human. He was also a cannibal, judging by the cracked limb bones and broken skulls found on the hearths.

Recent observations based on studies of Aleutians at Chaluka, Alaska, indicate that *Sinanthropus* was even closer to modern man than was previously believed. Laughlin observes that Paleo-Aleuts became more 'primitive' as time went on.[49] The series of skulls excavated at Chaluka demonstrated changes from a breadth less than 75% of its length in the Paleo-Aleut to a breadth more than 80% of its length in the Neo-Aleut. The skull vault also changed from a higher to a lower form. There were also changes in the occurrence of dental cusps and mandibular tori. All of these changes apparently occurred over the short time lapse of 4,000 years. In addition Laughlin points out that *Sinanthropus* displayed many traits found both in current Mongoloids and the related American Indians. For example, *Sinanthropus* had had an extra suture that separated the upper portion of the occipital into a separate triangular bone called the inca. This characteristic occurs not only in *Sinanthropus,* but also in present-day Mongoloids, American Indians, and even some Neanderthals. The frequency of occurrence varies. Although the above is not the common view of human paleontologists, the changes discussed by Laughlin and encompassed by the forms discussed so far could be well classed as being mere variations within mankind. Weidenreich[50] observed 12 traits in the *Sinanthropus* skulls that occur in Mongoloids of today and therefore held that it would be best to class *Sinanthropus* as *Homo sapiens erectus.* When this evidence is coupled with the large differences found among various living human groups, for example, Bushmen and Eskimos, one is justified in concluding that *Sinanthropus* could be classified as *Homo sapiens.* This then would also hold for *Pithecanthropus.*

Other *Homo erectus* forms are *Atlanthropus* (North Africa), and the Mauer mandible, also known as the Heidelberg jaw (Germany). A. N. Burkitt held that in regard to absolute size, the general type of tooth arch, the size and the shape of the ramus as well as the shape of the chin, parallels can be found in living races of mankind, and the possessor of the Heidelberg jaw.[51] Close agreement is found in occasional individuals of New Caledonia and the Loyalty Islands. Sarassin[52] and Arthur Thomson[53] also noted that dimensions of New Caledonia jaws sometimes show considerable similarities to Schoetensacks' figures for the Heidelberg jaw.[54]

Remains of a *Pithecanthropus* form, together with an abundant series of artifacts, have also been discovered in Israel in the Plain of Esdraelon. Flourine tests have caused the human finds to be divided into two different groups of different periods in time. Three of the skull fragments belong to *Pithecanthropus,* while the other two are more recent and seem to be related to other early *sapiens* finds. Implements associated with the finds are bifacial hand-axes and flint instruments, as well as fossils of animal bones.[55]

At this point mention should be made of the Swanscombe skull of England. This find is considered to be contemporary with *Homo erectus* forms, although without exception today considered to be *Homo sapiens.* Sir Wilfred Le Gros Clark has said: "Lastly, the evidence of the Swanscombe skull is of great importance because its antiquity is so well attested by stratigraphical, faunal, and archaeological evidence. . . . Only the parietal and occipital bones are available, though these are exceptionally well preserved. They show no distinctive Neanderthaloid features and in their dimensions and non-metrical characteristics are astonishingly similar to modern skulls."[56]

In addition to the Swanscombe skull, the Steinheim (Fig. A-9) is often considered as a modern-man type. Yet both of these forms predate Neanderthal man, according to accepted methods of dating today. There is an increasing agreement that all of the forms discussed so far—modern man, Neanderthal, and the pithecanthropine forms—are men in every sense of the word. When one considers that each of these is unmistakably associated with the manufacture and use of tools, as well as the controlled use of fire, it is clear that we are indeed dealing here with men.

A close long look at a representative collection of skulls of these forms also forces one to the conclusion that we have here various forms of men. This point of view can be found in Buettner-Janusch, Coon, Montagu, and others. It is to be noted that the various forms mentioned so far, do vary among each other, thus proving what has always been known, namely that man is capable of considerable variation. Henschen's work indicates the great variability of skulls of men living in historic times. Pericles, Erasmus, Swedenborg, and Toulouse-Lautrec all had abnormally shaped skulls.[57]

VII. The Australopithecines

Finally, let us consider the Australopithecines. To date the finds of this form consist of some 15 crania from five sites. Only three of these are relatively complete. There are also pieces of jaws and face(s) that some believe might add up to 100 individuals. If the contemporary animal remains are used as a criteria, most of the five sites were not contemporary. The various remains seem to sort themselves out into two populations. These fossil genera came to light with Dart's discovery of the Taungs infant skull in 1924. It was classified as *Australopithecus africanus.* The brain capacity was 494 cc. at 6 years of age, which has been extrapolated to 550 cc. for the adult. Other skulls were found at Sterkfontein, which were at first given the genus name *Plesianthropus* (see Fig. A-10). These have cranial capacities of 435 and 480 cc. Eight skulls were found at Swartkrans, but none is complete enough to do more than allow an estimate of 700 cc. There is considerable disagreement on these figures. But there is agreement that 700 cc. represents

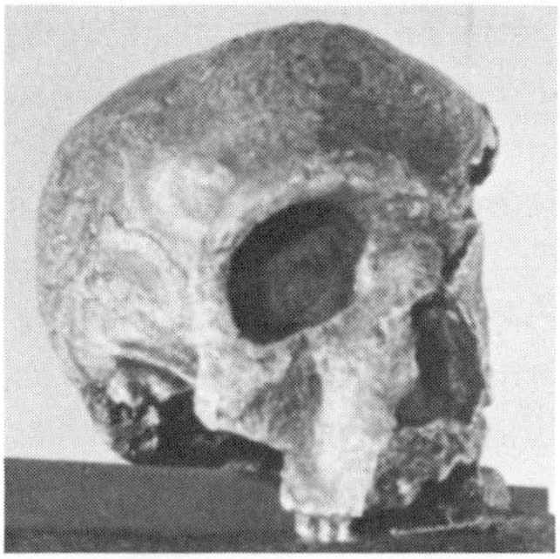

A.

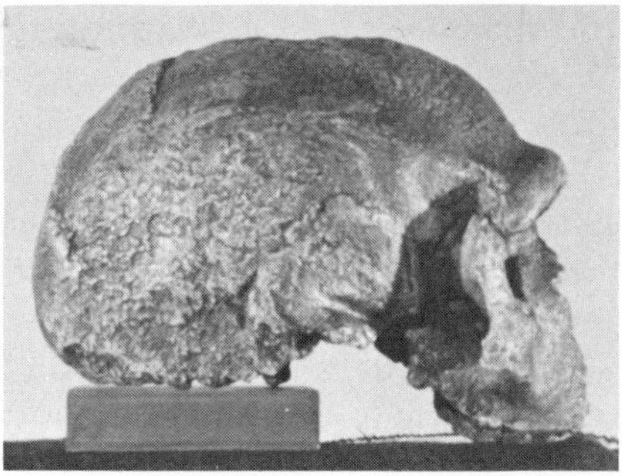

B.

Fig. A-9. Frontal (A) and profile (B) views of *Homo sapiens steinheimensis* (Steinheim Man).

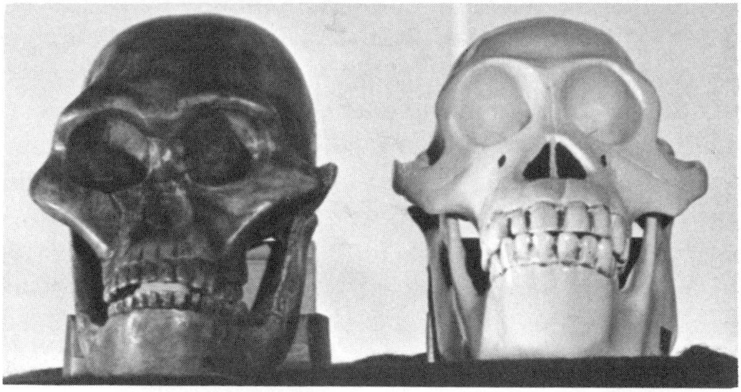

A.

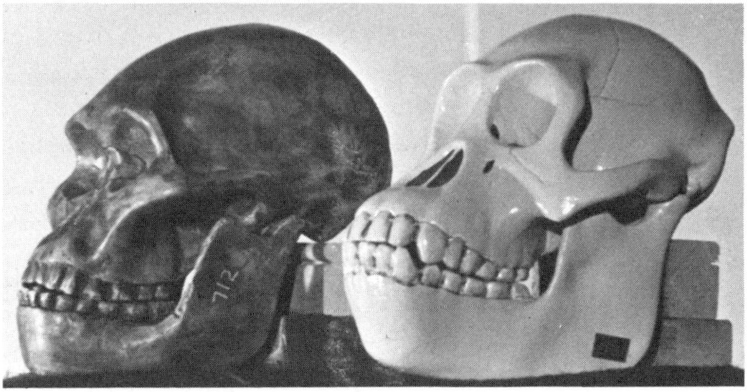

B.

Fig. A-10. Frontal (A) and diagonal (B) views of reconstructed *Plesianthropus (Australopithecus prometheus)* skull and cast of orang skull.

the maximum. The Swartkrans finds were classed as *Paranthropus* as were additional forms found at Kromdraai. All this adds up to a range in estimated brain size from 435 to 700 cc. The brain cases are considered by Coon (1962) to be human in form but apelike in size. Duyvenne de Wit, the South African paleontologist, has suggested that the Australopithecines might represent a race of *Homo* suffering from microcephaly.[58] Vallois (1957) considers the 200 cc. known gap between *Homo* forms and Australopithecines as a Rubicon which has never been crossed.

The Australopithecines (South African ape-men) today are usually classified as either *A. africanus* or *A. robustus.* Both are upright and bipedal. Robinson believes the two forms can be distinguished by many characters in the known material. All known *A. robustus* forms show a sagittal crest, which is absent in *A. africanus.* All the Australopithecines have greatly reduced canines and molars, no diastema, and both were tool users and therefore probably tool makers. Robinson reports that where *A. africanus* is found alone, tools are found. Where *A. africanus* and *A. robustus* are found, tools are also present. But where *A. robustus* is found alone, no tools are found. Straus considers *A. africanus* to be more human, but geologically older. On the other hand, he holds that *A. robustus* is less human, but geologically younger. Le Gros Clark holds that the total morphological pattern conforms to that of *Hominidae.* This recognition does not make them ancestral to *Homo sapiens.* Robinson lays great stress on a diet difference being responsible for the difference in skull architecture. *A. robustus* is considered to have been a plant eater, while *A. africanus* was omnivorous, with a considerable carnivorous element in his diet.[59] The herbivorous, diet is deduced from patterns of tooth wear.

There seems to be doubt in the minds of some anthropologists as to whether the Australopithecines are to be considered human. Wilfred Le Gros Clark said that "the terms 'man' and 'human' can only be applied to them [the Australopithecines] with some reserve, for there is no certain evidence that they possessed *any* of the special attributes which are commonly associated with the human beings of today."[60] (Italics mine). In addition, R. L. Lehrmann said: "Australopithecus was merely an upright intelligent ape, not a man. The small braincase bearing heavy ridges over the eyes, across the back and down the center was like that of any ape."[61] Also Ashley Montagu wrote: ". . . the skull form of all australopithecines is extremely apelike . . . . Such creatures could not have been directly ancestral to man . . . . the australopithecines show too many specialized and apelike characters to be either the direct ancestors of man or of the line that led to man."[62] (See Fig. A-10.)

One of the recent finds has been that of Leakey's "*Zinjanthropus* boisei" *(A. robustus* sp. (?)). This was found in Bed I, Olduvai Gorge, Tanganyika, East Africa, and reported by Leakey in 1959.

Another find of Leakey's has caused considerable stir. Leakey himself named this form *Homo habilis.* Since it was discovered in the same beds and at the same level (Bed I) as *Zinjanthropus,* it is considered contemporary with *Zinjanthropus.* This fact caused Leakey to change his opinion that *Zinjanthropus* was the originator of modern man. *Homo habilis* had sufficient resemblance to "almost" modern man so that Leakey felt justified in classifying him as *Homo* rather than in one of the other anthropological niches or genera. However, the remains are rather sparse, consisting of molars which are narrower than those of *Australopithecus,* a mandible (lower jaw) that is incomplete and the parietal bones of the skull. Tobias reconstructed the skull to give a 642 – 724 cc. capacity, which would surpass the *Australopithecus* range.[63] An unusually modern foot and a hand have also been recovered from the same bed. *Homo habilis* teeth do not show the wear patterns of a gritty diet as do those of *A. robustus.* Primitive stone tools are associated with *H. habilis. H. habilis* measurements are proportionally in the *H. sapiens* range.

To further complicate this picture, a pithecanthropine form called *Telanthropus capensis (H. erectus pithecanthropus?)* has also been discovered at Swartkrans. At present Leakey is suggesting that all three forms were contemporary.[64] He declared at the same time that this proposition would make all schemes of human evolutionary descent that had been written to date obsolete—including his own! There are workers in the field who disagree with this assessment of Leakey's. However, it would seem that the evidence is beginning to show that modern man (or forms closely resembling modern man) has been in existence as long as hominids have been known.

Two other African finds by L. S. B. Leakey should be mentioned. One was a human jaw of modern type found in Kanam and called by him *H. kanamensis.* It was found in association with *Dinotherium,* which also should place it in the Pliocene age. Since finding modern man in the Pliocene would be contrary to orthodox evolutionary theory, the discovery was immediately questioned. But Leakey changed the definition of the Pleistocene to include what British geologists would call the Upper Pliocene.[65] So in *Adams Ancestors* Leakey refers to the Kanam jaw as being Lower Pleistocene. The jaw has small teeth and a chin, which appear modern. Coon quotes P. V. Tobias as holding it had no true chin but a bone sarcoma grown over an old fracture. Hence Coon comfortably tucks it in among the Australopithecines.[66] Boule-Vallois also recognized the presence of a tumor, but holds that "enough is still visible, however, to show that its structure was that of the primitive types of modern man, and that while not pronounced, the mental protuberance existed."[67] The Kanjera finds, also by Leakey, consist of an incomplete skull and parts of two other skulls. These fragments all correspond to the long narrow heads with foreheads of modern man. A conference at Cambridge in 1933 concluded that both specimens—Kanam and Kanjera—were *Homo sapiens.*[68]

The best advice a creationist can follow was given recently by Dr. L. S. B. Leakey at a conference on the origin of man at the University of Chicago's Center for Continuing Education when he urged his fellow scientists "to refuse to accept theories as facts and look upon the origin of man with fresh eyes." At this meeting Leakey had announced that his finds indicated that *Zinjanthropus, Pithecanthropus* and *Homo habilis* types all lived at the same time! Furthermore, the evidence indicates that aberrant forms have coexisted with the conventional human type. Neanderthal man definitely was a "degenerate" form.

Patterson and Howells recently reported an interesting

find in northwest Kenya.[69] Here the elbow end of a humerus (upper arm) bone was found in sediments near the southern end of Lake Rudolf. These sediments were capped by a lava flow, which when dated by potassium-argon methods gave an age of approximately 3 million years. On the basis of fluorine methods, the bone agreed in age with other specimens from the sediments. The specimen is now named *Kanapoi Hominoid I.*

The bone was compared with the corresponding bones of a gorilla, an orangutan, and *Australopithecus robustus* by feeding the various dimensions into a computer. The comparison indicates that the fossil bone is clearly distinguishable from the corresponding bones in the apes. Likewise, comparisons indicated that *Australopithecus robustus* is less manlike than the *Kanapoi Hominoid I.* In fact the fragment of elbow falls very close to the modern human average. In the investigators' collection of human reference fragments the Kanapoi duplicated modern man almost exactly. Thus we again have the picture of a fossil similar to modern human, being older than the less human *Australopithecus* fossil. This again would seem to rule out a developmental tree running from *Australopithecus* forms, through *Pithecanthropus,* Neanderthal and Cro-Magnon forms, and culminating in a distinct modern man.

Summary and Conclusions

Primate fossils in general and human fossils in particular are comparatively rare and generally fragmentary. Even where a relatively complete skeleton is available, it gives very limited information about the outward appearance and character of the individual. The humanoid skeletons so far found can be assigned satisfactorily to two genera *(Homo* and *Australopithecus),* four species, and two subspecies. There is no objective reason for the multiplicity of names assigned to these remains. Of the four species, *Homo sapiens* and *Homo erectus* existed simultaneously, and so did *A. robustus* and *A. africanus.* There is preliminary evidence that a species of *Homo* coexisted with *Australopithecus.* If this is substantiated, it will show that the genus *Homo* is as old as the oldest known humanoid remains. The differentiation of species within *Homo* is dubious. There are living men with most or all of the skeletal characteristics of *Homo erectus*. The fossil evidence supports the conclusion that species of *Homo* similar or identical to *Homo sapiens* have existed since the initial appearance of humanoid fossils in the geological record. Therefore it may be concluded that fossil evidence offers no support for any schemes of the evolutionary descent of man, either within hominid genera or from primate ancestors.

Notes

1. Sir Arthur Keith, *Darwinism and Its Critics* (London: C. A. Watts & Co., 1935), p. 53.
2. George G. Simpson, "The World into Which Darwin Led Us," *Science*, cxxxi, p. 969.
3. Henry F. Osborn, *The Earth Speaks to Bryan* (New York: Charles Scribner's Sons, 1925), p. 2.
4. Arthur Keith, *Antiquity of Man* (London: Williams and Norgate Ltd., 1st ed. 1915, 2d ed. 1925), p. 441.
5. Francis Vere, *The Piltdown Fantasy* (London: Bassell, 1955).
6. Vincent E. Smith, ed. *Philosophical Problems in Biology* (Jamaica, N. Y.: St. John's University Press, 1966), pp. 119–20.
7. Marcellin Boulle and H. V. Vallois, *Fossil Men* (New York: Dryden Press, 1957), p. 3.
8. Gertrude Himmelfarb, *Darwin and the Darwinian Revolution* (London: Chatto and Windus, 1959), pp. 310–11.
9. R. Broom and C. W. Schepers, *The South-African Apeman—The Australopithecinae* (Pretoria: Transvaal Museum, 1946), p. 257.
10. *Bulletin.* American Ethnological Society, No. 52 (1912), p. 2.
11. Evan Shute, *Flaws in the Theory of Evolution* (London: Temside Press, Canada, 1961), pp. 208–10.
12. Paul L. De Vore, ed., *The Origin of Man* (Werner-Gren Foundation, 1965), p. 3.
13. *Encyclopaedia Britannica,* 14th ed. (1929), xv, 990.
14. "The Proper Study of Mankind as Man," *Nature,* Supplement, Sept. 5, 1959 (British Assn. Number), 38.
15. F. Walsche, "Thoughts Upon the Equation of Mind with Brain," *Brain,* lxxvi (1953), 1–18.
16. Carleton Coon, *The Story of Man* (New York: Knopf, 1954).
17. R. Linton, *The Tree of Culture* (New York: Knopf, 1955).
18. M. D. Sahlins, "The Origin of Society," *Scientific American* (Sept. 1960), p. 3 (reprint).
19. Loren Eiseley, "Fossil Man and Human Evolution," *Yearbook of Anthropology* (1955), p. 75.

20. D. O. Hebb and W. R. Thompson, "The Social Significance of Animal Studies," *Handbook of Social Psychology,* ed. G. Lindzey, I (Cambridge: Addison-Wesley, 1954).
21. Douglas Dewar, *The Transformist Illusion* (Murfreesboro, Tenn.: Dehoff, 1957), p. 25.
22. Vernon Reynolds, *The Apes* (New York: Dutton, 1967), pp. 95–96.
23. George G. Simpson, "The Meaning of Taxonomic Statements," *Classification and Human Evolution,* Sherwood L. Washburn, ed. (Chicago: Aldine, 1963), p. 21.
24. W. K. Gregory, M. Helman, and G. E. Lewis, *Fossil Anthropoids of the Yale-Cambridge India Expedition of 1935,* Carnegie Pub. 495 (Washington: 1938).
25. W. LeGros Clark and L. S. B. Leakey, *The Miocene Hominoidea of East Africa,* Fossil Mammals of Africa, No. 1 (London: British Museum, 1951).
26. John Buettner-Janusch, *Origins of Man* (New York: Wiley, 1966), pp. 123 to 126.
27. H. H. Woolland, *Science Progress,* xxiii, No. 129 (July 1938), p. 18.
28. Theodosius Dobzhansky, *Mankind Evolving* (Yale University Press, 1962), p. 171.
29. Simpson, p. 24.
30. Carleton Coon, *Origin of Races* (New York: Knopf, 1962), pp. 5–11.
31. *Toledo Blade,* Sec. A, p. 6. Reported by Ray Brunner, science ed., Nov. 21, 1965.
32. Eugene A. Golomshtok, *The Old Stone Age in European Russia,* private printing, diss., Philadelphia, 1938.
33. Hallan L. Movius, *Early Man and Pleistocene Stratigraphy in Southern and Eastern Asia,* xix, No. 3 (Cambridge: The Museum, 1944).
34. A. C. Blanc, "L'Homme fossile du Mont Circe." *L'Anthropologie,* XLIX (1939).
35. Theo. D. McCowan and Sir Arthur Keith, *The Stone Age of Mount Carmel II,* (Oxford: Clarendon, 1937), p. 11, 12.
36. M. L. Movius, "Notes on Tayacian Man," *American Anthropologist* (1948), pp. 365–67.
37. *Scientific American* (July 1948), p. 19.
38. W. E. Le Gros Clark, *The Fossil Evidence for Human Evolution,* 2d ed. (Chicago: University of Chicago Press, 1964).
39. G. H. R. von Koenigswald, *The Evolution of Man* (Ann Arbor: University of Michigan Press, 1962).
40. F. C. Howell, "The Pleistocene Glacial Ecology and the Evolution of Classic Neanderthal Man," *Southwestern Journal Anthropology,* VIII (1952), 377 to 410.
41. William S. Laughlin, "Eskimos and Aleuts; Their Origins and Evolution," *Science* 142 (Nov. 8, 1963), p. 633.
42. E. Dubois, *Pithecanthropus erectus, eine Menschenähnlich Übergangsform aus Java* (Batavia, 1894).
43. L. Salenka and N. Blankenhorn, *Die Pithecanthropus-Schichten auf Java,* (Leipzig, 1911).

44. R. A. M. Bergman and P. Karsten, "The Fluorine Content of Pithecanthropus and Other Specimens," *Mededelingen Koninklijke Akadinne von Wetenschappen Amsterdam.* lv (1952), No. 2, pp. 150–52.
45. Coon, pp. 399–400.
46. G. von Königswald, *Meeting Prehistoric Man.* (New York: Harper, 1956), p. 114.
47. Wilfred E. Le Gros Clark, *Man-Apes or Ape-Men?* (New York: Holt, Rinehart and Winston, 1967), p. 9.
48. J. T. Robinson, "Meganthropus, Australopithecines, and Hominids," *Am. J. Phys. Anthropol.* xi (1953), 1.
49. William Laughlin, p. 641.
50. F. Weidenreich, *Paleontol. Sinica* (1943), No. 10, pp. 127, 246, 256.
51. A. M. Burkitt, "Neanderthal Man and the Natives of New Caledonia," *Nature,* cxxii, No. 3704, pp. 474–75.
52. Sarassin, *Altas zur Anthropologie der Neu-Caledoner und Loyalty Insulaner,* 1922.
53. Arthur Thomson, *Journal of Anatomy,* L.
54. O. Schoetensack, *Der Unterkiefer des Homo heidelbergensis* (Leipzig, 1908).
55. *Archaeology,* xxi (Jan. 1968), 65.
56. Sir Wilfred Le Gros Clark, *Antiquity* (March 1954), p. 4.
57. Folke Henschen, *The Human Skull* (London: Thames and Hudson, 1965), pp. 30–32.
58. Duyvenne de Wit, *The Paleontological Record and the Origin of Man* (privately pub., 1963), p. 24.
59. J. T. Robinson, *The Origin and Adaptive Radiation of the Australopithecines — Evolution and Hominisation.* G. Kurth, ed., (Stuttgart: Fischer, 1962), pp. 123 to 127.
60. W. E. Le Gros Clark (1964), p. 172.
61. R. L. Lehrmann, *The Long Road to Man* (New York: Basic Books, 1961), p. 115.
62. Ashley Montagu, *Man: His First Million Years* (Yonkers, N. Y.: World Pub., 1957), pp. 51–52.
63. P. V. Tobias, "Cranial Capacity of Zinjanthropus and other Australopithecines," *Nature,* cxcvii (1963), 743–46.
64. Paul L. De Vore, p. 11.
65. L. S. B. Leakey, *Adam's Ancestors* (New York: Harper & Bros., 1944), p. 25.
66. Coon, p. 296.
67. Boule and Valois, p. 443.
68. "Early Human Remains in East Africa," *Man* (April 1933).
69. Bryan Patterson and W. W. Howells, "Hominid Humeral Fragment from Early Pleistocene of Northwest Kenya," *Science,* clvi (April 7, 1967), pp. 64 to 66.

Appendix A

Living things, with the exception of the viruses, are classified according to the following scheme:

- * Kingdom—Animalia or Plantae
  - * Phylum (if animal) or Division (if plant)
    - Subphylum
      - * Class
        - * Order
          - Suborder
            - Infraorder
              - Superfamily
                - Tribe (used primarily in insects)
                  - * Family
                    - * Genus (genera—pl.)
                      - * Species

* Indicates the hierarchial level usually used. The other ranks are used where some investigator deems it necessary further to split large groups.

Appendix B

George G. Simpson's proposed classification of the super-family Hominoidea

- Superfamily Hominoidea
  - Family Pongidae
    - Subfamily Hylobatinae
      - Pliopithecus (extinct)
      - Hylobates (gibbon)
    - Subfamily Dryopithecus (extinct)
      - Dryopithecus
      - Proconsul (tentative)
      - Ramapithecus (tentative)
      - Kenyapithecus (tentative)
    - Subfamily Ponginae
      - Pongo (orang-utan)
      - Pan (chimpanzee)
      - Gorilla
  - Family Oreopithecidae (extinct)
    - Apidium
    - Oreopithecus
  - Family Hominidae
    - Australopithecus (extinct)
    - Homo

—From George G. Simpson, "The Meaning of Taxonomic Statements," *Classification and Human Evolution,* S. L. Washburn, ed. (Chicago: Aldine Pub. Co., 1963), p. 29.

Appendix C

Taken from Douglas Dewar, *The Transformist Illusion* (Murfreesboro, Tenn.: Dehoff Publications, 1957), p. 140.

Evolution [noncreation] Theories Regarding the Origin of Man *(Homo Sapiens)*

Class I. Man descended from anthropoid ape or from an ancestor of an anthropoid ape.

Group I

All races of men are derived from the same species of anthropoid ape (monophyletic origin).

(a) From an unknown kind of ape (C. Darwin)
(b) From a *Dryopithecus*-like ape (E. Haeckel)
(c) From a *Sivapithecus*-like ape (G. E. Pilgrim)
(d) From an *Australopithecus*-like ape (R. Broom, G. Schepers, W. Le Gros Clark, later view) (Dewar considered *Australopithecus* an ape)
(e) From a gorilloid ape (W. K. Gregory)
(f) From a brachiating ape (A. Keith, later view)

Group II

Different races of men are derived from different kinds of apes (polyphyletic origin).

(a) White man and chimpanzee derived from one kind of ape; Negroes and gorillas from a second kind of ape; Mongolians and orangs from a third kind of ape (Ardt, Kurz, Crookshank).
(b) The primary races of man now living, which should be deemed species, not races, have arisen independently from different species in different continents (Gates).

Group III

Man and anthropoid apes are derived from a common ancestor and are separate from all other primates.

(a) From a Simian of later date than *Propliopithecus* (W. K. Gregory (later opinion), Elliot Smith (later view), L. H. D. Buxton, W. L. Straus)
(b) From *Propliopithecus* (W. K. Gregory (earlier view), L. S. B. Leakey)
(c) Man branched off from the lemur stem before the appearance of *Propliopithecus* (A. Keith).

Group IV

Man descended from a lemuroid without passing through an ape stage (Haacke).

Class II. Man evolved from a tarsioid ancestor.

Group I

Man passed through an anthropoid stage (Elliot Smith [earlier view], E. Hooten).

Group II

Man did not pass through an anthropoid stage (F. Wood Jones).

Class III. Man evolved from a New World (Platyrrhine) monkey (Hubrecht).

Class IV. Man evolved from a Prototarsioid (W. Le Gros Clark).

Class V. Man evolved from a reservoir of generalized Archae-primata, from which arose in the Eocene bipedal *Anthropomorpha primitiva,* which gave birth to *Pithecoid homunculi* from which man emerged (G. Schepera).

Class VI. Man evolved from an upright ancestor early in the Tertiary period (H. F. Osborn).

Class VII. The human stock branched off from the main primate stock before the lemurs and tarsiers evolved (Sera), branching as follows:

(1) represented by the Polynesians but by no anthropoid ape
(2) represented by the Mongols and the orang
(3) represented by the Caucasians and the Persians but no anthropoids
(4) represented by the Europeans and the fossil *Dryopithecus*
(5) represented by Negroes, the chimpanzee, and most gibbons
(6) represented by the Bushmen, the Andamanese, the gorilla, and the syndactylous gibbons

Class VIII. Man branched off from the other vertebrates as far back as Paleocene times; the group to which he belongs had opposable thumbs and great toes (H. Klaatsch).

Class IX. Man is derived from the most primitive mammal, and his line did not pass through a lemur or tarsier or anthropoid stage (Westenhofer).

Class X. The six types of man cited by Sera above each evolved independently of one another from different lumps of amorphous matter in the sea, which independently formed themselves into multicellular animals, each of which, by processes like those that occur in the development of embryos, followed by changes such as occur in larvae, eventually developed each into a different type of man (Sergi).

SECTION V

Noah's Flood

10 • The Biblical Account of the Flood

FRED KRAMER

In Genesis chapters 6–8 the Bible records the story of a great flood, brought on by God as a result of the all but universal wickedness of mankind. In this flood all men and beasts were destroyed with the exception of Noah and his family and pairs of all land animals that Noah had taken into the ark which he had built in response to a command from God.

From ancient times observant Bible readers have pondered the vast effects which the Flood must have had on the surface of the earth and what traces it may have left which may be observable today.

The Jewish philosopher Philo, who lived in Alexandria in Egypt during the first century of the Christian era, speculated on this question. It was discussed by the church fathers Tertullian, Chrysostom, and St. Augustine.

Martin Luther discusses the possible effects of the Noachian flood on the surface of the earth in his commentary on the Book of Genesis as follows:

> How does He [God] bring about the destruction? It is obvious that He takes the element water and destroys everything. The force with which this element is wont to rage is well known. Even though the air may be pestilential, it does not always contaminate trees and roots. But water not only demolishes everything and not only tears out trees and roots, but it carries away the very surface of the earth and alters the soil so that even the most fertile fields are ruined by the saltiness of the earth and by the sand. This, then, was the destruction of the first world.[1]

However it was not only theologians who were interested in the possible effects of the flood on the surface of the earth. During the 18th and much of the 19th century the so-called flood theory of geology was accepted by many geologists and other scientists. The flood theory of geology was compatible with a larger geological school of thought known as catastrophism.[2]

About the middle of the 19th century the theory of uniformitarianism became popular and seriously challenged catastrophism, and with it the Noachian deluge as being of any significance for geology. It is not our purpose to present the history of the struggle between catastrophism and the flood theory of geology on the one hand and uniformitarianism on the other, but rather to show what happened in connection with this struggle to understand the flood story in Scripture itself.

The Noachian flood, which up to this time had been used by many geologists to explain the sedimentary rock strata with their multitude of fossils, was eliminated as a geological factor. Others who were not willing to go to this extent, sought for one reason or another to make the Genesis flood a relatively minor incident in the history of the earth. Hugh Miller, a Scottish geologist of the 19th century, who sought to harmonize geological science with the Scriptures, argues that the flood described in Genesis must have covered only a part of the globe, from the fact, as he conceived it, that the ark described in Genesis could under no circumstances have held a pair of every known species of animal.[3]

While attempts to view the Noachian deluge as anything less than universal were initially stoutly resisted by theologians, the assumption of a partial or local flood eventually was accepted by a very large proportion of Old Testament scholars. Archaeologists of a higher critical bent have also contributed to this development.

Through the work of archaeologists many ancient records have been discovered, some of them containing stories of a flood that bears remarkable similarities to the Biblical story of the deluge, though very different from this story in other respects. Such stories have been found in Assyria, Babylonia, and Sumeria.[4]

With the discovery and use of these texts by Old Testament scholars is connected a shift in the interpretation of sections of the Old Testament.

For 18 centuries Christians had read the Bible as history. This meant that also the story of the Flood was history. According to traditional Christian hermeneutics the Flood was understood to have been universal, covering the whole earth.

According to this understanding it seemed to be not only permissible but necessary to draw conclusions also in the matter of scientific questions from the flood account. As the geological features of the earth became better known the flood theory of geology gradually developed.

With the coming of the higher literary and historical criticism during the 18th and 19th centuries it became fashionable to brand many things in the Bible as myth. Along with the story of creation, the story of the Noachian flood was considered mythical. What is more, the story was considered to have been copied from the myths of Babylon, Assyria, and Sumeria. However, since that time there has been a considerable modification of this theory among Old Testament scholars. As was brought out in our discussion of the creation account earlier in this volume it has become customary to consider these stories not myth, but rather saga, that is, accounts that may not be history as a modern historian would write it, but which nevertheless are based on actual happenings.

The literary *genre* of saga, however, is said to call for a new hermeneutic. According to this hermeneutic the Biblical story of the flood is interpreted as an account of a very limited flood which has been built up out of all proportion. Gerhard von Rad discusses the relationship between the Biblical story of the flood and the other Near Eastern flood stories as follows:

> Concerning the relationship of the Biblical tradition to the Babylonian story of the flood as we have it above all in the Gilgamesh epic, the accounts have now, 40 years after the high point of the Babel-Bible dispute, been all but closed. A relationship of material between the two accounts certainly exists, but exegetes have ceased entirely to assume a dependence of the Biblical

> tradition on the Babylonian period. Both accounts are independent developments of an even more ancient tradition which on its part may have come out of Sumeria. When Israel entered Canaan it found there a tradition of the Flood and incorporated it in its faith.[5]

The Anchor Bible, which is dominated by the higher criticism, has the following to say on the origin of the account of the Flood in Genesis, with a strong implication that the historical kernel behind the "saga" is a limited, even local flood.

> The ultimate inspiration for the Mesopotamian cycle of Flood narratives can only be a matter of guesswork at this time. Perhaps the best chance of a likely solution lies in the recent disclosures concerning the geological background of Lower Mesopotamia (cf. J. M. Lees and N. L. Falcon, "The Geological History of the Mesopotamian Plains," *Geographical Journal,* 118 [1952], 24 to 39). It now appears that not very long ago, as geological ages are reckoned, waters from the Persian Gulf submerged a large coastland area, owing probably to a sudden rise in the sea level. If that rise was precipitated by extraordinary undersea eruptions, the same phenomenon could also have brought on extremely heavy rains, the whole leaving an indelible impression on the survivors. All this, however, must remain in the realm of speculation.[6]

The part which more recent archaeologists have played in downgrading the Noachian deluge from a universal to a merely local flood is illustrated by the following example. In 1929 C. Leonard Wooley, an archaeologist, announced that he had discovered what he considered to be positive archaeological evidence of the Genesis flood. Digging on the site of the ancient city of Ur, in Mesopotamia, Wooley had caused a deep shaft to be sunk through a pile of rubbish outside what had been the city wall. The purpose was to dig down to virgin soil, where no artifacts should any longer be found. In the words of Harold Peake:

> At last, when the workmen had dug down to the level of the surrounding plain, they reached a clean water

> laid clay containing no fragments of pottery, or any foreign substance except a piece of the fossilized bone of some animal. The workmen believed that they had reached the bottom, and that this was virgin soil, but Wooley was not satisfied that this was so. The pit was carried down deeper, through eight feet of solid, clean and unstratified clay, and below this he found a stratum, rich in flint chips and cores, and quantities of pottery fragments, some like the plain types found above, while the majority were of painted ware . . . Still deeper he sunk the shaft, finding more pottery, some plain and some painted, then fragments of a new painted ware not met with before, and at the very bottom a burnt brick of a totally new type. Lastly, when they had dug down to a few feet above the present level of the Persian Gulf, they came to the clean river silt of the original island, and were satisfied that they had reached virgin soil. Here, it appeared, was direct proof of the existence of the Flood, and that the painted ware, as had been suspected, was of antediluvian date.[7]

Peake describes other layers of fresh water-laid clays that have been found in Mesopotamia, and he concludes that there were a number of floods, one of them having been described in the Scripture as the Noachian flood.

He sums up his conclusions as follows:

> The Flood, then, was one of those normal inundations which are apt to occur from time to time in the lower reaches of the valleys of large rivers, such as the Mississippi, the Indus, or the Hoang-ho. It was probably not so extensive, or even so destructive, as the great Mississippi flood of a few years ago, or the great inundation of the Hoang-ho in China which is said to have been recorded by Yu about 2260 B. C. Unless the flood that deposited the clay at Ur was greater than that which laid down stratum D at Kish, the river did not rise more than twenty feet, or extend very far on either side of its normal channel.[7]

Such are the views of the Biblical story of the Flood expressed by at least some Biblical archaeologists and higher literary and historical critics of the Bible. Their views, while they may be of no interest whatsoever to professional geologists, are not in conflict with the views of uniformitarian geologists. However, there is no room in uniformitarian geology for a universal flood which left traces all over the earth or greatly changed the earth's crust. All geological phenomena are considered to be the result of geological processes. The occurrence of local catastrophies by earthquake and minor flood and volcanism are by no means denied. However, the processes are assumed to work in a uniform manner, though the uniformity may be observable only when the processes are watched over a long period of time.

An Examination of the Biblical Deluge Story

Against these views of geologists, archaeologists, and higher critics, the text itself seems to speak clearly, not of a locally limited but of a universal flood.

1. Scripture presents the Flood as an act of God made necessary by the wickedness of all mankind.

> Gen. 6:5-7: And God saw that the wickedness of man was great in the earth, and that every imagination of the thoughts of his heart was only evil continually. And it repented the Lord that He had made man on the earth, and it grieved Him at His heart. And the Lord said, I will destroy man whom I have created from the face of the earth; both man, and beast, and the creeping thing, and the fowls of the air; for it repenteth Me that I have made them.

Everything here speaks of a universal situation on earth, calling for a universal remedy, in this case a universal flood.

2. God commanded Noah, who alone with his family had found grace in God's sight, to build an ark in which he and his family and a pair of animals of every kind might be preserved alive (Gen. 6:14 ff.). It is not our purpose here to discuss the adequacy of the ark for such a task, or to argue with those of a past generation who, because they believed in the fixity

of species, as the concept "species" was then understood, believed that the ark was far too small to accommodate all necessary animals. Suffice it to say that the Biblical term "kind" (Hebrew—"min") used in the Genesis creation and flood accounts is a comprehensive term which is larger than species or genus (Lev. 11:13-19). This weakens arguments against the reality of the flood account based on the capacity of the ark.

It should be pointed out that if the flood was merely a local affair, covering perhaps one major river valley, then there was no need to preserve either man or beast, because a depopulated valley would soon be peopled again from the outside.

3. The language of the Scripture used to describe the Flood appears to speak plainly of a universal flood.

The source of the waters of the Flood is described in Gen. 7:11-12. We quote the passage in a number of modern translations:

> MOFFATT: On that day the fountains of the great abyss all burst, and the sluices of heaven were opened.
>
> SMITH-GOODSPEED: On that very day the fountains of the great abyss were all broken open, and the windows of the heavens were opened.
>
> REVISED STANDARD VERSION: On that day all the fountains of the great deep burst forth, and the windows of the heavens were opened.
>
> JERUSALEM BIBLE: That very day all the springs of the great deep broke through and the sluices of heaven opened.
>
> ANCHOR BIBLE: On that day "All the fountains of the great deep burst forth, And the sluices in the sky broke open."

It is worth noting that there are no essential differences in these translations. It is further worth noting that the Anchor Bible prints these verses as poetry. This is helpful for a correct understanding of the text. Instead of looking for a mythical source of waters inside the earth, the reader should understand that the text would say in language of great poetic beauty that the ocean poured its waters upon the land, and that rain fell in torrents. Scripture does not tell us what geological forces, perhaps worldwide volcanic disturbances, "broke open the fountains of the great abyss," or what meteorological forces caused "the windows of heaven" to be opened. But it does record the fact that these things happened and that these are the two sources of the waters of the Noachian deluge.

This explanation is in harmony with the rest of Scripture. The great deep manifestly is the ocean. Originally, according to Gen. 1:2, the whole earth was covered with water and this is called "the deep," but according to Gen. 1:9, God caused the waters under the heaven to be gathered together into one place, the seas. This is called thereafter "the great deep."

The universality of the flood appears plainly expressed in Gen. 7:19:

> And the waters prevailed exceedingly upon the earth; and all the high hills, that were under the whole heaven, were covered. Fifteen cubits upward did the waters prevail; and the mountains were covered. And all flesh died that moved upon the earth, both of fowl and of cattle and of beast and of every creeping thing that creepeth upon the earth and every man; all in whose nostrils was the breath of life, of all that was in the dry land died. (KJV)

The universality of the flood is implied furthermore in Gen. 8:21-22 where, at the sacrifice of Noah,

> The Lord said in His heart, I will not again curse the ground any more for man's sake; for the imagination of man's heart is evil from his youth; neither will I again smite any more every thing living, as I have done. While the earth remaineth, seedtime and harvest and cold and heat and summer and winter and day and night shall not cease.

These are not remarks suited to a local flood. They are appropriate only for a flood that was universal, involving the whole earth.

This is also the implication of Gen. 9:19, where the Bible

remarks concerning the three sons of Noah: "These are the three sons of Noah; and of them was the whole earth overspread."

The New Testament, no less than the Old, indicates that the Noachian deluge was universal. St. Peter says concerning the scoffers of his day, who refused to believe that Christ would return to judgment: "They deliberately ignore this fact, that by the word of God heavens existed long ago, and an earth formed out of water and by means of water, through which the world that then existed was deluged with water and perished." (2 Peter 3:5-6 RSV)

These words speak of the destruction, not of a small area of land in Mesopotamia, but of the world that then existed. They describe a universal flood and universal destruction.

Geological Implications of a Universal Flood

Assuming that we have read the flood story correctly, what changes might be expected to have been made on the surface of the earth by such an event?

Proponents of the old flood theory of geology were inclined to attribute many, if not most, of the earth's fossils containing strata to the Noachian deluge.

Believers in the Biblical flood story today, better schooled in geological science than were flood geologists of former generations, will avoid the obvious mistakes made by earlier flood geologists. It is impossible to identify specific geological phenomena as having been produced by the Noachian deluge. Much happened before the deluge; much happened after it. The Scripture does not purport to give us a record of all that took place. Believers in the Scripture should study the Biblical record and the record in the book of nature, and compare the two diligently. Above all it is the duty of theologians to read their Bible carefully and accurately, and not to make it say what it does not say.

Nowhere does the Bible identify certain specific geological phenomena as the result of the Flood. A careful reading of the Scripture reveals that the Bible stresses, not building, but destruction on the part of the Flood. Gen. 6:7 (KJV): "And the Lord said, I will destroy man whom I have created from the face of the earth; both man, and beast, and the creeping thing, and the fowls of the air." Gen. 6:13: "And God said unto Noah, the end of all flesh has come before Me; for the earth is filled with violence through them; and behold, I will destroy them with the earth."

This passage is basic for an understanding of the effects of the Flood. God threatened that He would destroy man *with* the earth. The Scripture does not say in what sense the earth is to be destroyed, but it does say that the earth is to share in the destruction which God would bring to mankind through the Flood.

Assuming that the Flood was universal, as the language of Scripture indicates, the Flood was eminently suited to carry out God's purpose of destruction.

As noted earlier, Scripture indicates that there was a twofold source of the waters of the Noachian deluge. "The fountains of the great deep [were] broken up and the windows of heaven were opened," Gen. 7:11. Violent rains for 40 days and 40 nights, coupled with immense tidal waves eventually covering the whole earth, certainly would have sufficed to drown land animals and simultaneously to produce destruction such as cannot be realized even by those who have witnessed the devastation accomplished by major floods.

If we have read the Biblical account correctly, the Flood reached its greatest height at the end of 40 days and 40 nights, and "all the high hills that were under the whole heaven, were covered." Gen. 7:24: "And the waters prevailed upon the earth an hundred and fifty days." We understand this to mean that until the end of the 150 days the Flood was at its greatest height. For 40 days it had risen, until the earth was covered; for an additional 110 days it remained at its greatest height, neither rising nor falling.

Flood geologists believed that it was during these 110 days that many of the earth's strata had been laid down from materials that had been held in suspension in the waters of the Flood. Their arguments are however speculative. Scripture does not speak on the topic of strata formation, but stresses the mission of destruction of the Flood. This mission was served admirably not only by the manner in which the waters came, according to the Scripture, but also by the manner in which they left the earth.

Considering the amount of water involved in the Noachian deluge (according to the Biblical account), the waters disappeared with surprising speed.

> And God remembered Noah, and every living thing, and all the cattle that was with him in the ark; and God made a wind to pass over the earth, and the waters asswaged; the fountains also of the deep and the windows of heaven were stopped, and the rain from heaven was restrained; and the waters returned from off the earth continually; and after the end of the one hundred and fifty days the waters were abated. And the ark rested in the seventh month on the seventeenth day of the month, upon the mountains of Ararat. And the waters decreased continually until the tenth month; in the tenth month, on the first day of the month, were the tops of the mountains seen. Gen. 8:1-5.

An examination of the figures in this passage shows that the waters of the Deluge disappeared from the earth very rapidly. The statement in verse 3 indicates that it was at that point, 150 days after the opening of the windows of heaven and the breaking up of the fountains of the great deep, that the waters began to recede.

The date when the ark rested on the mountains of Ararat is given as the 7th month, on the 17th day. Comparing this with the date of the beginning of the Flood, Gen. 7:11, one finds that the ark stopped on the mountains of Ararat on the very day that the floods started to recede. After about 73 days, according to Gen. 8:5, the tops of the mountains were seen. According to Gen. 8:13, "It came to pass in the six hundredth and first year, in the first month, the first day of the month, the waters were dried up from off the earth." It took, therefore, 5 months and 13 days for the water which had covered the whole earth, including the tops of the mountains, to subside. This is a very short time for so much water to disappear.

To assume that this vast amount of water evaporated

seems to be in harmony with neither the text nor with any known law of nature. Rather, one would assume that the waters, which had largely come from the ocean, returned to the ocean. Major physical changes which Scripture does not describe and which we do not pretend to understand must nevertheless have taken place to account for the rapid subsiding of so great a flood. One is led to think of major changes in the earth's crust, the rise and fall of land masses, etc.

The rapid return of the waters from the face of the earth accords well with God's purpose in sending the flood, to "destroy man with the earth." Water, moving even at a relatively slow speed of a few miles per hour, can work tremendous havoc, as the recurring floods in river valleys have shown time and again. So great a mass of water as that represented by a universal flood rushing with great speed to the ocean would work great destruction on the surface of the earth. Major changes in the topography would surely be expected.

The question whether or not the Noachian flood may have left permanent traces in the earth's crust cannot be answered categorically. Geologists have not been able to identify such traces today with certainty. The Noachian flood was an act of God which is not susceptible to our research and verification. Christians believe it, because the Bible, which they revere as God's Word, teaches it. They see in the story not only the account of a great catastrophe but beyond that a powerful account of man's sin, of God's wrath against wickedness, and of His saving grace to those who believe in Him.

Notes

1. Luther's Works, II: *Lectures on Genesis,* chs. 6–14, American Edition (Saint Louis: Concordia Publishing House, 1960), 66.
2. For a history of the flood theory of geology see Byron Nelson, *The Deluge Story in Stone* (Minneapolis: Augsburg Publishing House, 1953), 190 pp. Writers in the area of geology, who held and defended the flood theory of geology in recent times were George McCready Price, *The Modern Flood Theory of Geology* (New York: Fleming H. Revell Co., 1935); and Alfred Rehwinkel, *The Flood* (St. Louis: Concordia Publishing House, 1951). The flood theory of geology (with considerable modification) is also set forth in Henry M. Morris and John C. Whitcomb, Jr., *The Genesis Flood* (Philadelphia: The Presbyterian and Reformed Publishing Co., 1962).

3. *The Life and Works of Hugh Miller, Vol. II: Testimony of the Rocks; Old Red Sandstones* (New York: Robert Carter & Brothers, 1882), pp. 320–61.
4. These flood stories may be found in the following works: N. K. Sanders, *The Epic of Gilgamesh* (Baltimore: Penguin Books, 1960), 129 pp.; Harold Peake, *The Flood, New Light on an Old Story* (London: Kegan Paul, Trench, Trubner & Co., Ltd., 1930); British Museum, *The Babylonian Story of the Deluge and the Epic of Gilgamesh, 1920;* Albert T. Clary, *A Hebrew Deluge Story in Cuneiform* (New Haven: Yale University Press, 1922), 83 pp.; *Ancient Near Eastern Texts,* ed. James Pritchard (Princeton: Princeton University Press, 1955), pp. 42–44.
5. Gerhard von Rad, *Genesis* (Goettingen: Vandenhoeck & Ruprecht, 1949), p. 101. Trans. John H. Marks (Westminster Press), © 1961, by W. L. Jenkins. Used by permission.
6. From *Genesis* (Anchor Bible) trans. and ed. by E. A. Speiser. Copyright © 1964 by Doubleday & Co., Inc.
7. Harold Peake, *The Flood, New Light on an Old Story* (London: Keegan Paul, Trench, Trubner & Co., Ltd., 1930), pp. 96–97.
8. Ibid.

11 • Geology and the Flood

PAUL C. TYCHSEN

Throughout the 18th century and well into the 19th, many scientists and theologians were convinced that the Deluge was responsible for most of the fossiliferous strata of the earth. Baron Georges Cuvier (1769–1832) championed the doctrine of catastrophism. This belief in the catastrophic doctrine stood unchallenged for some time, until the time of Charles Lyell (1797–1875) who enthusiastically accepted the Hutton-Playfair doctrine of progressive geologic change.

Although Lyell erroneously assumed that geologic processes have always acted at the same rate, he is considered to be the "high priest of uniformitarianism"—a doctrine subscribed to by the majority of current geologists. Possibly the best expression of what the geologist means by uniformitarianism is the maxim that "the present is the key to the past." More specifically, we believe that the laws of nature, as we witness them in operation at the present time, furnish the best clues as to how and why things occurred in the dim past. Indeed, the principle does not require that specific features of the environment, such as running water, wind, and ice, have always been uniform in the amount or degree of erosion accomplished, but allows for considerable variation throughout geologic time.

An adherent of absolute uniformitarianism would believe that identical causes produce identical results. This position would be difficult to prove, since time and space relationships are continually changing. Accordingly the geologist assumes that every event of geologic significance is quite unique and will not be repeated in its exact setting. Perhaps a better way to express the idea of uniformitarianiam is to call attention to the Law of Similar Conditions, which declares that similar causes must produce similar results, and that the interpretation of observed results will yield reliable explanations of their causes. One should note that the law calls for similar and not identical conditions. Thus it tends to avoid the weakness implicit in the theory of a strict uniformitarianiam. The principle of uniformitarianism does not imply that the present and the past are identical. Furthermore, no restrictions whatsoever are placed upon the kind of geologic process that operated in the past nor on the rate at which the process operated. Cataclysmic events occur in space as evidenced by exploding-type stars and crater-bearing planets. Simply stated, the present offers the most reliable clues to thinking about the past. It is under this canopy that the present-day geologist seeks the truth.

One objective of science is the acquisition and organization of factual knowledge. Considerable information, for example, has been garnered as to the extent and frequency with which lands were covered by shallow seas in the past. A specific example may suffice to illustrate. If the North American continent were depressed approximately 600 feet, the Mississippi valley as well as a considerable portion of the Coastal Plain would be covered with a shallow sea. Florida would be reduced to a mere submarine bank. Assuming that the seas remained over the area for some time, sediment such as sand or silt would spread over much of the area. This would be particularly true in the shallow water. Many shells would be buried. Some would ultimately become fossils of marine life. Along the shores, beach gravels, wave-cut cliffs, wave-cut terraces, and well-defined strand lines would eventually appear. The entire shoreline would resemble many of the strands now commonplace throughout the world. Depending upon the local conditions, and given sufficient time, vast sheets of limestone might be deposited in the somewhat deeper waters. The limestones could be fossiliferous and hence offer telltale evidence of their marine origin.

If the continent were subsequently uplifted or if the sea level subsided, the marine deposits and the strand lines would provide evidence of former submergence. The fossils would give clues as to the type of environment which had existed.

By plotting this information on a map, the limits of vanished seas could be reasonably well established. Throughout much of geologic time, shallow or epeiric seas have covered portions of continents. The evidence indicates a marine origin for the vast deposits piled one on top of the other in many portions of the earth. Frequently they are separated by nonmarine deposits.

If one examines the geologic record, he will find that specific periods of geologic time were characterized by very extensive floods, which covered considerable portions of entire continents. The Ordovician period, for example, witnessed a flood sufficiently large to cover over half the North American continent—reducing it to a group of large islands practically awash in the sprawling sea. From the record, no other flood in geologic time has been quite so extensive—at least not in North America. In fact this period marked the most extensive known encroachment of the seas upon the land masses of the world. Geologists believe that this maximum extent flood occurred approximately between 440 to 500 million years ago.

The remaining periods in the Paleozoic age all witnessed floods of lesser extent in a rhythmic-like pattern. In fact the Paleozoic era has often been characterized as a time of continually transgressing and regressing seas. The Mesozoic era similarly continued the trend. During the termination of this era, specifically during the so-called Cretaceous period, the extent of submergence was one of the greatest the earth has known. This particular period culminated approximately 70 million years ago, according to estimates. During the ensuing Cenozoic era (the most recent era) the lands gradually became more emergent, and the present-day landscape unfurled. The latter part of the Cenozoic witnessed the ice age, during which approximately one third of the earth's land surface was covered by ice of considerable thickness.

If the former ice sheets could be restored, sea levels would be lowered by some 300 feet. The shoreline would shift seaward approximately to the present 50-fathom line. The evidence seems clear now that postglacial climates reached a maximum warmth between 4,000 and 6,000 years ago and have since cooled to the present time. During this period of deglaciation meltwaters were quite confined compared to the Ordovician and Cretaceous periods.

We find, therefore, that the record, particularly that of the sedimentary rocks, is replete with information concerning the particular environments which existed from time to time. Fossil content, color of rocks, thickness of formations, sedimentary structures, grain size and shape, and finally mineral or chemical composition enable the geologist to suggest the particular environment in which these features developed.

For example, red, red-brown, and purple colors are characteristic of most nonmarine sediments which were deposited on the land surface and came into contact with the atmosphere. The colors result from the oxidation of iron. Fossils are very useful in distinguishing between marine and nonmarine sedimentary rocks. Specific groups of animals are exclusively marine today. When we find fossil representatives of these forms in a formation, we assume the formation to be of marine origin.

Geologists believe that thick, widespread units of limestone could only have developed beneath shallow seas. Certain rock structures, such as ripple marks, record times in history when loose sea-bottom sediment or desert sands were wafted about by currents, waves, or winds. These were ultimately compacted and cemented and now offer specific evidence of a past environment. Modern-day environments demonstrate many of the same characteristics and structures and thus enable the geologist to utilize the present as the key to the past.

The traditional Biblical date for the Flood, as computed in the Ussher chronology, is approximately 2350 B. C., some 4,300 years ago. This date, however, is subject to the criticisms advanced earlier in this book by Kramer. Regardless of the exact date, the Biblical account states that great quantities of water descended upon the earth without ceasing for 40 days and nights and remained on the land surface for some 371 days. The account in Gen. 7:19, 20 (KJV) states:

> And the waters prevailed exceedingly upon the earth, and all the high hills that were under the whole heaven were covered. Fifteen cubits upwards did the waters prevail, and the mountains were covered.

The duration of the Pleistocene epoch is said to have been anywhere from three-quarter million to two million years.

If one attempts now to pinpoint the occurrence of the Deluge by correlating it with commonly accepted conclusions of geology, Noah's flood would necessarily be confined to the waning stages of this epoch or the beginnings of the Recent (or Holocene) epoch.

Fairbridge (1960) has presented a graph (see Fig. 1) showing the constant rise of sea level from a time approximately 17,000 years ago to the present. The graph indicates a most marked rise in sea level to a time approximately 6,000 years ago. Fairbridge states that this marked rise indicates the most rapid upsurge of the sea identified in the geologic record. He states:

> The greatest and fastest rise yet discovered in the geological record reached its crest about 6,000 years ago. The cumulative incursion of the sea flooded low-lying coastal lands in every part of the world. This was the deluge that drowned the homes and troubled the legends of the ancients. The flood of the sea was joined by floodwaters brought down from the highlands by rivers. In the worldwide climatic shift that brought on and reinforced the melting of the glacier, climatic belts shifted everywhere on earth except near the equator. Regions of the temperate zone where the recorded history of mankind was just beginning became noticeably milder and wetter. Archaeological evidence in the valley of the Tigris and the Euphrates and geological evidence in the valley of the Mississippi testify to calamitous and spectacular inundations.[1]

At this point it may be well to recall that the Deluge is a commonplace phenomenon in the folklore of many ancient groups. Greek legend, Babylonian scripture, and Hindu literature all attest to the presence of a flood. These varied legends cannot be accepted by geologists as unchallenged proof of an inundation. However, it can be argued that geological science may possibly produce evidence of the very phenomena which inspired the ancients to record the flood in their literature. Such evidence, at least in part, may be apparent on the graph in Figure 1. The reader will note that the sea level curve for the past 6,000 years has been quite stable, indicating but slight recession of the water. Fairbridge notes that the variation of sea level during this span of time has been of the magnitude of 10 or 12 feet above or below the present sea level. Certainly the lands throughout the world would have witnessed the effects of such a marked rise in sea level.

Centers of trade and civilization some 6,000 years ago were located along river valleys and at seaports where transportation junction points offered man an opportunity for survival. Rise in sea level at this time would be particularly noticeable along the shorelines characterized by shallow depths immediately offshore and where the coastline was relatively straight. Additional quantities of water were being contributed by rivers such as the Tigris and Euphrates whose valleys witnessed frequent floods. Considerable land about the Caspian is below the general level of the Black Sea and the Mediterranean, and one of the earthquake zones in the world extends east and north of the Persian Gulf and continues across Mesopotamia. Subsidence, however slow, of parts of this structurally weak region may well have initiated further flooding of extensive areas.

To an observer in Biblical times, the world was primarily confined to an area bounded in the north by the Black Sea, in the east by the region immediately beyond the Tigris, in the south by the Persian Gulf, and in the west by islands of the eastern Mediterranean. With such limited geographic information, communications, and scientific equipment, attempts to accurately assess the extent of the Flood would have been virtually impossible. This has led some to suggest that Noah's flood may merely have been a local affair and not world wide. However, Holy Scriptures are quite explicit about it having covered the entire earth. (Cf. Kramer's discussion earlier in this section.)

One might conclude furthermore that if water had remained on the earth's surface for merely a year or so, as recorded in Scripture, little evidence, if any, would be left. Strand lines demand considerable time before the landscape bears evidence of their existence, and the amount of sedimentation taking place during a single year on shallow sea floors would scarcely be noticeable. Leet and Judson (1966) state that:

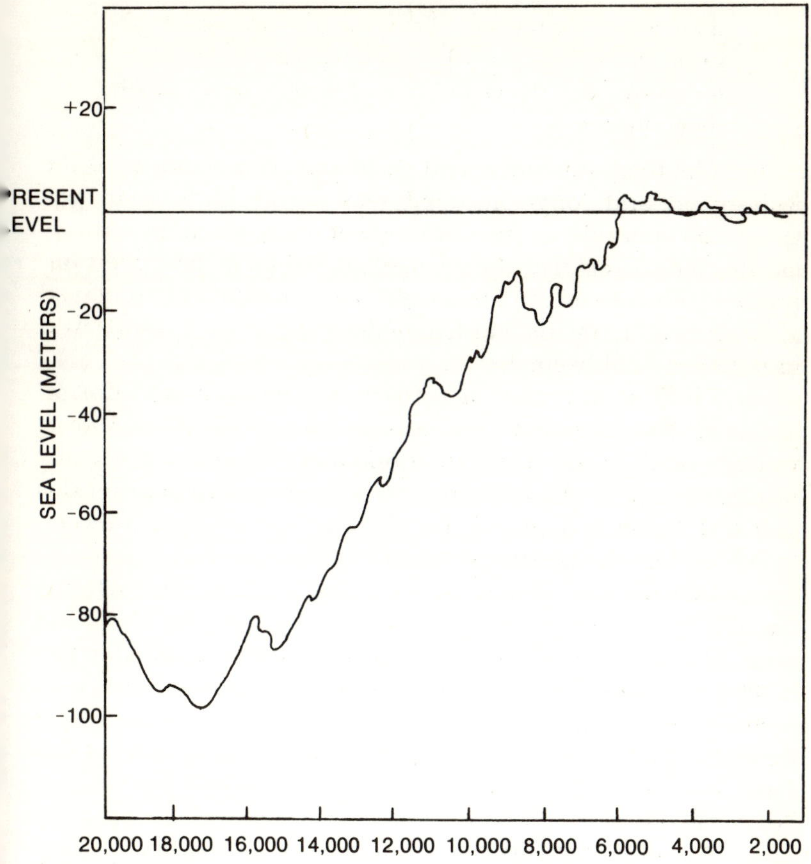

Fig. 1 (modified after graph by Fairbridge, 1960). From Rhodes W. Fairbridge, "The Changing Level of the Sea," *Scientific American,* May 1960, p. 76,

Graph indicating marked rise in sea level from about 17,000 years ago to an unusually high level approximately 6,000 years ago. This marked rise is one of the most rapid upsurges of sea level recorded in geologic history.

> Most sediments are deposited in the shallow waters of the continental shelves or on the slopes leading down to the deep sea. Very few sediments get to the deep sea floor, where the rate of sedimentation on average seems to be 0.5 inches per 1000 years or less. In contrast, on shelves and slopes the rate appears to be 10 to 20 times this rate.[2]

The thick limestone and shale units characteristic of the widespread and long-continued seas of the Ordovician and Cretaceous periods, as previously mentioned, would be entirely lacking, and even if a thin veneer of sediment had been deposited, subsequent erosion would have undoubtedly removed all evidence. Little or no sedimentary trace of a short-lived inundation would remain.

This line of reasoning is from the viewpoint of uniformitarianism and does not take into account the fantastic effects which would result from an inundation of the entire globe in a period of 40 days. Again, see Kramer's discussion on this point. However it is entirely possible that the evidence has been obliterated by the passing millenia.

In summary it may be said that geologic research has discovered records of many great floods. It has also shown an unusual rise in the world's water level at a time approximately 6,000 years ago. But it is not possible at this point in time to identify any of these phenomena from the past with Noah's flood. Geology simply does not provide us with an answer of this type. Nor does the Bible enable us to establish the date of Noah's flood.

It would therefore seem best to allow Noah's flood to be a concern of theologians. Certainly geologists can neither prove nor disprove it. The believer does not doubt that God in a miraculous act could have inundated the entire globe. From this point he moves on to ponder the great lesson of sin and grace which the story of Noah and his world provides for modern man.

NOTES

1. Rhodes W. Fairbridge, "The Changing Level of the Sea," *Scientific American*, May 1960, p. 75.
2. L. Don Leet and Sheldon Judson, *Physical Geology* (New Jersey: Prentice-Hall, 1965), p. 240.

Epilogue

Paul A. Zimmerman

The preceding chapters have ranged over many topics, both scientific and theological. To what conclusions have they led us?

Of course they have not answered all the questions about creation. No one on the symposium was presumptuous enough to think they would. Perhaps they even raised more questions than they answered. Notwithstanding, certain things *do* emerge—things that are most helpful to the man who strives to be faithful both to his Bible and to his science.

First, there is the mystery of it all! You dare not forget or neglect the mystery. Man who inquires into the ultimate—the absolute beginning of all things—is confronted wherever he turns by vast patches of impenetrable mystery. It all happened so very long ago. No one was present to observe save God and His angels. So much has changed since then—changed again and again and again! And the Bible says so very little about many things we would like to know. Yes, wherever you turn there are the puzzles, the lack of data, the awesome silence, the mystery.

Only fools give to speculation the weight of proven fact. When one talks of "The Beginning," one must humbly bow, over and over. From time to time we have a glimpse of clear sky, but then the clouds again cover the mystery. This is an area of intellectual activity where theologians and scientists alike had best stand with shoes removed as on holy ground.

Hand in hand with this first observation there comes the second. God worked in creation in a special way. He works now, too. But it is different today. Now, except for a miracle when He pleases, He works through the laws of nature which He Himself established. But how was it at the beginning, when God first spoke and began to create? No one knows or could comprehend if he were told, for we too are a part of that creation, thinking creatures—but creatures none the less. Let none then dictate what God could or would do. Even less let men presume to deny God's existence, because God does not behave as they prescribe. God is the greatest mystery!

Beyond this, the men of the Symposium engaged in long and repeated dialogue; they hurled conflicting ideas like thunderbolts; they wrestled intellectually with no holds barred, but they never felt tempted to deny the Word God has given us in the Holy Scriptures. They talked of errors in science and in theology, but not of error in the Bible. They were as strong at the end as in the beginning in the conviction that God does not lie in His Word. They rejected as disastrous compromise the expedient of accusing the Bible of error. Nor did they find ground for accusing the Scriptures of containing myth. By God's grace and Spirit they were able to operate as modern men in the same framework of reverence for revealed truth that has always marked the church. They did not solve all the problems, but they were content to believe that before God who knows all, the truths of nature and of Holy Scripture are in sweet harmony.

The men of the Symposium examined the foundations of science. They admired their strength and they noted the limitations. They evaluated men of science as honest men pursuing their research but noted them also as men subject to human frailties—even as are theologians. Science cannot become a sacred cow. Nor do men of science want it to be.

Beyond this they noted that when science deals with the past, it operates on a different basis than when it deals with the present. Conclusions based on uniformitarianism may be faulty. Witness the words of the Icelandic geologist, Sigurdur Thorarinsson's writing of the island of Surtsey, born of a volcanic action in 1963: "An Icelander who has studied geology and geomorphology at foreign universities is later taught by experience in his own homeland that the time scale he had been trained to attach to geological developments is misleading when assessments are made of the forces—constructive and destructive—which have moulded and are still moulding the face of Iceland. What elsewhere may take thousands of years, may be accomplished here in our century. All the same he is amazed whenever he comes to Surtsey, because the same development may take a few weeks or even a few days here!" *

Despite the limitations imposed on those who study the past, an impressive amount of cumulative evidence points to the earth being far older than 6,000 years, as Ussher postulated. But we have seen that Ussher's dates of creation cannot be regarded as dates established in the Holy Scriptures.

So far as evolution is concerned, the symposium agreed that forms of life have varied through the ages. Witness the vast variety today of even so common a species as the dog. But Scripture does not say that the originally created kinds could not vary. It does limit the variation to the boundaries of the "kind," but it does not define these boundaries.

Moreover, change and variation in themselves surely do not prove evolution. The long, long line of ascent from inorganic chemicals to life, to primitive forms, to higher forms, to man—this remains the unproved hypothesis of evolution. Many scientists believe it firmly. Others do not accept it. Those who *do* believe it, do just that—they believe in a scientific dogma. The strength of that belief is attested by the vigor and ridicule with which they attack those who challenge the sacred dogma. One is permitted to attack this or that phase of the theory, but to challenge the concept of evolution from nonlife to man is strictly forbidden.

The Bible, both in Old and New Testament, is very specific about Adam and Eve. They were created by God in a special act. They were truly human from the beginning. They were not the descendants of earlier lower forms of life. Because of this, the chapter on human evolution is important. Man may have varied physically through the ages, but the fossil record does not prove his descent from other forms of life. Man has always been man.

For those who doubt the Biblical story of man's creation, let it be pointed out that the Biblical account of man's nature is beyond challenge. Surely, also in our day, man—the greedy, the lustful, the cruel, the sinner, has again proved he is all that God says he is: Fallen from his created righteousness, he is the most dangerous of the beasts until God's love touches him and he is reborn through the Gospel. Today, as in ancient times, man needs Jesus Christ, his Savior. This is the truly important fact.

Man wants to deny God's very existence. The clay denies the hands of the potter that shaped him. The creature wants to preempt the role of Creator. Only by God's grace in Christ can man be reborn and return to the state of blessed holiness and peace he had at creation.

So the Rock Symposium ends. It was an association of men who, bound together by a common faith in their Savior, probed a bit deeper into the mysteries of creation. They join in pointing out the fact that the greatest mystery, that God loved man in Christ, has been clearly revealed so that even a child can see it.

May modern man in his pride never allow his frustrations about other mysteries cause him to pass by this so great a salvation!

Note

* Thorarinsson, Sigurdur. *Surtsey: The New Island in the North Atlantic.* Almenna Bokafelagio, 1964, p. 52.

Glossary

Amphibian—Cold-blooded animal that breathes by means of gills in the early stages and by lungs in the later stages of life.

Analogia Scripturae—Latin phrase meaning the "analogy of Scripture," the concept that a given passage must be interpreted in the light of the entire Bible.

Baculum—Bone in penis, for example, raccoon.

Brachiopod—Marine animal having two unequal shells or valves each of which is bilaterally symmetrical.

Carnivorous—Organism with a meat diet.

Catastrophism—The concept that the differences between the plants and animals found as fossils in the various rock strata and those living today are due to a series of catastrophies which wiped out all life in a given area so that subsequently different plants and animals came in from another area of the world.

Convergence—The concept that similarities are due not to descent from a common ancestor but from adaptation to a similar environment.

Copernican Theory—In astronomy the concept that the sun is the center of the solar system and that the earth and the planets move around it.

Cosmic radiation—Highly energetic particles bombarding the earth from unknown sources in outer space. The effect of these rays is to produce reactions in the upper atmosphere, one of which converts nitrogen^{14} to carbon^{14}.

Cosmogony—Theory of the origin of the universe.

Crossopterygian—A primitive fish which had lungs as well as gills.

Dental formula—$\frac{\text{incisors}}{\text{incisors}} - \frac{\text{canine}}{\text{canine}} - \frac{\text{premolars}}{\text{premolars}} - \frac{\text{molars}}{\text{molars}}$

Diastema—Gap between canine and incisor teeth.

Dripstone—Cave deposit.

Echinodermata—A phylum of spiny-skinned animals, exclusively marine, nearly all of whom have radially and five-rayed symmetry.

Exegete—Biblical interpreter.

Fossa—Cavity or depression in a bone.

Fossil—Hardened remains of plant or animal life of some previous geological period.

Genre—A kind or type of literature, for example, a myth, an epic, a straightforward historical account, a poem.

Geostrophic cycle—The concept that mountains are raised, and destroyed by erosion—particularly that rocks formerly beneath the oceans have been raised into mountains.

Herbivorous—Organism with a vegetable diet.

Hermeneutics—The science of Biblical interpretation.

Hominid—Human form.

Index Fossil—A fossil characteristic of a given age, the discovery of which in a given rock is believed to clearly date the rock as belonging to that particular age.

Invertebrates—Animals without backbone.

Lapilli—Fine spherules of volcanic ash ranging up to ¼ in diameter. In volcanic terms ash is very fine dust.

Limestone—A sedimentary type rock—consisting chiefly of calcium carbonate.

Lithology—Character of the rock relating to minerals and texture.

Loess—Fine sand deposited by wind, characteristically found near the edge of former glaciers.

Lutheran Confessions—Theological position papers of the Lutheran Church in the 16th century, subscribed to also today as true expositions of Holy Scripture.

Mastoid—Region behind ear.

Microcephaly—Abnormally small head.

Mollusc—Group of animals characterized by an external shell of which the snail is an example.

Neo – Prefix denoting recent.

Niche – Level.

Omnivorous – Organism feeding on both plants and animals.

Paleo – Prefix denoting ancient.

Paleontology – Area of biology which deals with the plant and animal life of past geological ages.

Palynology – Study of remains of ancient pollen grains and spores.

Parity principle – It was formerly thought that nature has no preference for 'right-handedness' as opposed to 'left-handedness.' This is now shown to be false. The results have been a profound reconsideration of the nature of the atom.

Pectoral – Front upper chest region.

Pelagic ooze – Extremely fine grained mud accumulating on the floor of the deep oceans.

Phlogiston – A substance believed to be released from a combustible material when it burned. Thus it was believed that wood when it burned gave off a substance called "phlogiston." Today we believe that combustion represents the combination of oxygen with some material in the combustible substance.

Phyla – Plural of phylum.

Phylogenetic Tree – A diagram to represent the way in which different plants and animals are supposed to have evolved.

Phylum – A group of closely related classes of animals or plants.

Phytosaur – A Triassic age reptile adapted to life on the land; resembled modern gavials (Indian crocodiles) in appearance.

Plutonic – Originating at depth in the earth.

Post-orbital (constrictions) – Indentations over temple.

Potassium-argon (method) – Radiogenic dating method used for rocks.

Proto – Prefix denoting early.

Protozoa – A phylum consisting of simple one-celled animals.

Protuberance—Projection.

Protrusible—Projecting.

Ptolemaic Theory—In astronomy the concept, now rejected, that the earth was the center of the universe, that it did not move, and that the sun and the planets revolved around it.

Quantum mechanics—Concept also linked with Einstein which shows that energy cannot be cut up into arbitrarily small increments, but occurs in discrete packets or quanta. Linked with this is the concept that small systems are not completely deterministic in behavior, but act according to probability rules. Quantum mechanics has not yet been successfully reconciled with relativity.

Relativity—Concept linked with the name of Einstein showing that distances and times depend on the state of the observer. The validation of this principle destroyed the classical mechanics of Newton. It is important at very large distances and high velocities.

Reptile—Cold-blooded vertebrate (animal with backbone).

Ripple mark—Small, wavelike forms produced in unconsolidated material (sediment) by wind or water.

Sarcoma—Cancer.

Sedes doctrinae—Latin for "seat of doctrine" or principal location in the Bible where a certain doctrine is set forth.

Sediment—Material like sand, silt, or clay—in suspension in water or recently deposited from streams, lakes, or seas.

Sedimentary—Descriptive term for rock formed of sediment.

Sensus literalis Scripturae unus est—Latin phrase meaning "Scripture has one intended meaning."

Septuagint—Ancient Greek translation of the Hebrew Old Testament.

Shale—A fine-grained rock formed from clay.

Silt—An unconsolidated clastic sediment finer than sand.

Sola Scriptura—Latin phrase meaning "Scripture alone."

Steroscopic—Binocular vision.

Strand—Synonymous with beach.

Stratified—Formed or lying in beds, strata, or layers.

Supra orbital (ridges)—Brow ridges.

Symbol—Synonym for doctrinal confession.

Tectonic—Relating to movements of the earth in response to internal forces.

Terrestrial—Consisting of or pertaining to the land as distinguished from the sea or water.

Thallophyta—Subkingdom of plants; body undifferentiated without roots, stems, or leaves; relatively unimportant as fossils.

Till moraine—Deposits of sand and boulders formed by glaciers either at their snout or sides (moraine), or during melting of the ice (till).

Trilobite—A primitive, extinct crustacean abundant during earlier Paleozoic periods. Characterized by segmented body divided into three lobes.

Turbidity current—Flow of thin mud under water.—Often triggered by earthquakes in mud banks with surprisingly low slopes. They are a major means of transporting material in the ocean.

Unconformity—The plane between a series of stratified rocks which have been tipped up and bevelled by erosion, and an overlying series of stratified rocks.

Unidirectional evolution—An evolution which admits of no return to an earlier state. According to strict uniformitarianism, the physical state of the earth should oscillate within fixed limits about some average condition.

Uniformitarianism—The concept that differences between fossil plants and animals and those alive today are due to gradual change over a long period of time.

Uniformity—The concept that the laws of science hold true in time and space, that the same scientific laws held in the past as hold today and that these laws apply everywhere in the universe.

10/22/70
RG